Understanding Your Church's Curriculum

Understanding Your Church's Curriculum

Revised Edition

HOWARD P. COLSON
AND
RAYMOND M. RIGDON

BROADMAN PRESS
Nashville, Tennessee

© Copyright 1981 • Broadman Press

4232-01

ISBN: 0-8054-3201-9

Dewey Decimal Classification: 268.6

Subject Heading: RELIGIOUS EDUCATION—CURRICULA

Library of Congress Catalog Card Number: 80-67351

Printed in the United States of America

To

Our Colleagues with Whom We Shared

Responsibility in Developing

Southern Baptist Curriculum Design

and to

Our Fellow Workers in

The Cooperative Curriculum Project

Contents

Foreword

Helpful books on curriculum are few and far between. For several years the previous edition of this book has been the only volume available that did justice to Protestant curriculum development in both theory and practice. This new edition, up-to-date and substantially rewritten, with additional foundational material and with close attention to the refinement of the basic model of learning, is encouraging and welcome. Its publication should spark new interest in and debate on curriculum theory and new concern for the theological and educational authority of the curriculum as a tool for Christian education.

What has taken place in curriculum in the eleven years since the publication of the first edition? The concept of curriculum has itself come under severe criticism, but has emerged from that criticism with a stronger place in the church's life. Christian education cannot be reduced to a "happening." We have become more than ever convinced that a responsible church cannot do without an educational plan. At the same time our conviction has grown that such a plan must represent the full life, work, and belief of the church as it attempts to maintain faithful worship, witness, and service in the modern world. We have found, too, that we are required to be more knowledgeable about educational matters and more selective in our use of educational models.

These years have also brought a shift in curriculum focus to the congregation. There has never been any question but that if it did not happen in the local church, it did not happen! Yet the prevailing belief was that somehow nationally designed programs and materials would take root and flower on the local scene without much help. We now see that the congregation has to be the center of educational planning, and that when the congregation has assayed its mission, needs, and objectives, it is in a position to select or design the curriculum that it needs. National bodies have responded with a greater richness and variety of materials. Accompanying this new trend is a stepping-up of attention to local planning and supervision. Both of these are well-reflected in the new edition of this book.

Generally, curriculum development has been proceeding forward in a steady way. The various denominations and denominational consortiums have continued to take the curriculum task seriously and have sought to improve their work by benefiting both from experience and from research. Notably, there is evidence of a growing social conscience and world consciousness in the curriculum, as well as more attention to the new person in Christ and to the church as Christ's body. The Bible is not so likely to be chopped up and segmented in contemporary curriculum as it is to be taken in terms of the integrity of its whole and parts. One notes a humanization of the curriculum that, perhaps paradoxically, seems to have become possible because of its renewed emphasis upon transcendence.

Sadly, there is less give-and-take among Protestant curriculum people today than there was eleven years ago. One major denomination last year issued a basic policy statement that for the first time in fifty years failed to make explicit commitment to such give-and-take. How long a creative and productive approach to curriculum can be maintained without the benefits of this critical and constructive curriculum activity is, of course, a serious question.

There are four essential considerations in Christian education when it comes to curriculum planning and design. First, there is the authentic Christian faith, which determines the character and substance of the educational experience. By "the authentic Christian faith" is meant, in this connection, the Christian gospel and the Christian life. The experience that the Christian faith provides is an informing, saving, sustaining, and growing one. Second, there is the self, the learner. But the self is misunderstood if it is thought of in exclusively individual terms, for the self, in addition to being an individual reality, is a corporate reality, as evidenced in the fact of the church. Furthermore, the individual and corporate learner is to be understood both existentially and developmentally. There is both a basic "now" about learning, and a lifelong continuity to it. Third, there is the context of the culture, which acts as a basis for how learning takes place. As curriculum is built in Appalachia, in urban America, among Asian-Americans, and in the Caribbean, there are necessary differences in educational approach, because people in these cultures learn differently. Fourth, there is the language spoken, for the language spoken is our means of communication. The language that we speak in Christian education reflects our faith, our culture, and our individual experience, and is often hard to equate with the language that the learner speaks out of his or her faith, culture, and experience. What coordinates these four, and makes a curriculum possible, is the Christian faith experience—found, lived, expressed, and shared in the church.

Howard Colson and Raymond Rigdon know these things, and have put them well in *Understanding Your Church's Curriculum*. Because of this, this new edition of the book will be read, pondered, argued, and used by all who are deeply concerned that the church not falter in the days ahead for lack of an adequate educational plan.

D. Campbell Wyckoff
Princeton Theological Seminary
Princeton, New Jersey
April 12, 1980

Introduction

The decade of the eighties may be one of the most exciting periods in the history of Christian education.

During the past two decades, several major curriculum studies have generated new insights in learning in relation to the great realities of the Christian faith. These new insights have been used in developing new kinds of curriculum designs and resources. These new designs and resources now are stimulating renewed interest in Christian education in the churches.

By God's grace, we, by reason of our personal involvement in curriculum development, have been in the midst of this curriculum revolution. We participated in the Cooperative Curriculum Project, from inception to completion, during 1960-64. During 1965-69, we had companion leadership roles in developing the curriculum design and resource materials which were introduced in Southern Baptist churches in 1970. Throughout the seventies, we further refined and validated many of the principles and approaches we had learned in the earlier experiences as we worked together in reorganizing and expanding the Seminary Extension curriculum of the six seminaries of the Southern Baptist Convention. Out of these rich experiences, we have written, and more recently revised, this book.

Our purpose is to describe some of the changes taking place and to interpret curriculum in the sense in which the term is generally used today. We compare curriculum with a giant tree, the roots of which go deep into the earth and provide sustenance to the visible trunk, branches, and leaves. In early chapters, we analyze the design of the curriculum, which is comparable to the roots of the tree. Later we describe visible aspects of the curriculum which are in evidence in almost every church.

We believe that leaders in Christian education need a basic understanding of the design and scope of the curriculum. Therefore, we are writing to pastors, ministers of education, more thoughtful lay church leaders, denominational workers, and seminarians of all evangelical faiths.

For many of the insights reflected in this book, we should like to express our personal indebtedness to our fellow workers in the program organizations of the Southern Baptist Convention and to our colleagues in the Cooperative Curriculum Project. We hereby express our indebtedness to both and our appreciation for the privilege of quoting from documents which they generated.

Although we are writing to Christian educators of all Protestant faiths, we confess a special interest in our Southern Baptist colleagues who are doing further work on the curriculum design which we had a part in developing a decade ago. We invite their special attention to the summary of their base design, appearing in Appendix A, which includes the revisions they have made up to this time.

We send forth this book in the conviction that Christian teaching and training continue to be two of the most effective means of interpreting the gospel. Our prayer is that this volume shall make a worthy contribution to the advancement of Christian education in the eighties.

1
Why Churches Must Educate

In a day of vast and sweeping changes, when many people no longer regard as important some of the values highly prized by former generations, what is the true status of Christian education?

Many people—some of them in the churches—feel that this enterprise has no particular significance. Of course if they are right, a great deal of effort is being wasted. Many millions of dollars are still being spent on it every year, and several million volunteer workers give freely of their time and energy to it every week. Is all of this worthwhile? Or is there need to reevaluate what is being done? If churches still need to engage in the teaching ministry, just why should they?

We suggest five inescapable reasons why churches must educate. Let us proceed to examine them.

Christ Expects It

Jesus Christ, both by example and explicit command, has emphasized for all time the importance of the teaching ministry. During his earthly mission he was called "teacher" more frequently than he was called by any other designation. Eighty-nine times the four Gospels refer to him as a teacher; they refer to him as a preacher only twelve times. Often, of course, his teaching and his preaching merged, but the work of teaching was always central in everything he did.

Jesus taught great crowds—on the hillsides, by the lake, in the synagogues. He used wayside opportunities to teach lone individuals. He especially gave long hours and days to the private training of the twelve.

The chief characteristic of his teaching was the way he pressed home God's truth to the inmost souls of people. His teaching and his mission were inseparable. He came and he taught in order to bring persons into right relations with God and with one another.

Unquestionably our Lord intended that his church should be a teaching church. The religion he founded is a teaching religion. This becomes explicit in the Great Commission: "Full authority in heaven and on earth has been given to me. Go then and make disciples of all the nations, baptize them into the name of the Father, the Son, and the Holy Spirit, and teach them to practice all the commands that I have given you" (Matt. 28:18-19, Williams). Every part of that commission calls for a program of teaching and training.

The first step is the making of disciples. The very name means "learners" and implies an educational process. Even the King James translation of the first part of verse 19 is suggestive, for what better way can be found of making disciples than teaching persons the truth as it is in Jesus?

With respect to baptism, the act itself is a visual aid in teaching the redemptive meaning of the Savior's death, burial, and resurrection. This meaning needs to be interpreted to every baptismal candidate, but we are often guilty of failure at this point.

We are also guilty of failure at the final stage of the Commission. To teach disciples to practice all that Jesus has commanded calls for a continuing program involving every member of the church. Some persons seem to view conversion and baptism as the end of a process rather than as the beginning. But when churches fail to follow through on their educational responsibilities, new members remain babes in Christ, and the consequences are serious—for them, for their church, and for the cause of Christ.

Some churches may think they have fulfilled the demands of the Great Commission simply because they support the various missionary causes of their denomination, but in actuality they have not met its demands until they have committed themselves to an adequate teaching ministry in their own local community.

The Gospel Demands It

Churches are the custodians of a divine revelation. They have a gospel to share. Its central reality is the fact that God in Christ has provided eternal redemption for sinners. That is good news, and good news must be shared.

The gospel has power to transform life. When persons accept and believe it, they become new creatures; old things pass away, all things become new. The gospel prepares persons for living in fellowship with God both here and hereafter.

All Christians believe that the gospel ought to be preached; many do not seem to realize that it ought also to be taught. But every reason for preaching God's redemptive message is at the same time *a reason for teaching it.* In fact, some aspects of divine revelation can be communicated more effectively through teaching than through preaching.

Revelation and education are not unrelated entities; they belong together; they are inseparable. Teaching the gospel is an essential way of propagating it. This is a compelling reason why churches must teach. Christian education is valid and relevant today because of the nature of the gospel.

History Proves It

The New Testament church was a teaching-learning fellowship. Teaching was its very lifeblood. In characterizing the Christian community as it functioned after the great ingathering at Pentecost, Luke wrote that "they were continually devoting themselves to the instruction given by the apostles, to the fellowship, to the breaking of bread, and to the prayers" (Acts 2:42, author's translation). By this process of sharing, the church assimilated the new converts to its own distinctive way of life and worked to bring them to maturity in Christian character and service.

Later, when the apostle Paul became the leading exponent of the new faith, he devoted himself assiduously to a teaching ministry (cf. Acts 11:25-26; 18:11). He taught in person and he also taught through his writings. Every one of his epistles was a teaching document, intended for the instruction of his converts.

The history of the Christian movement from apostolic days to the present reveals that every great period of revival has been accompanied by a fresh emphasis on teaching. There is not room here to review that history; we shall simply note two outstanding examples of the principle.

During the Dark Ages, the evangelical vitality of the church was sadly lacking. It was a time when both general education and Christian education had sunk to very low levels; in fact, they scarcely existed. But then came the Protestant Reformation and the accompanying Revival of Learning. The connection was not accidental. The Protestant movement led to the establishment of many institutions of learning. Within the local churches, the system of catechetical instruction which had been prominent in an earlier day came to life again. Once more the gospel was preached from the pulpit, a large element of it, significantly, taking the form of teaching.

The other example is from eighteenth-century England. Religion and morals had again reached a very low level. But then came the Wesleyan revival. Many people do not realize it, but one of the major reasons for the phenomenal growth of Methodism was the educational program which John Wesley so wisely planned and so earnestly promoted. Had it not been for that program, who knows what might have become of his movement? Over the long years it might have amounted to no more than the movement which came into being through the preaching of George Whitefield, Wesley's gifted contemporary.

Whitefield, we are told, was in some ways an even more powerful preacher than Wesley, yet his movement survives today only in a small and little-known religious group in England called the Countess of Huntingdon's Connexion. What made the difference? Whitefield had no organized plan for developing his converts; his whole emphasis was on preaching. But with Wesley's well-organized educational plan, especially the so-called class meeting, his movement grew to worldwide proportions. Whitefield had no such plan and his movement dwindled.

History confirms the conviction that developing a church into what a church should be demands Christian education. It also confirms the fact that such a program need in no way conflict with other aspects of a church's responsibility. Rather, a program of teaching and training undergirds the entire work of the church and provides a means whereby the other functions can be more effectively carried out. Through the educational ministry, all of the other work becomes more dynamic and fruitful.

People Need It

The needs of individual persons call for a Christian educational ministry. Wherever you find mature, well-balanced, witnessing Christians, you know that back of their fine development lies some effective teaching and training. There is no quick, easy way to grow stalwart Christians. They must be developed by a long, slow, sometimes painful educational process. To recognize that fact is not to discount the Holy Spirit's work, for he himself is a teacher, ever making use of the educational process to accomplish his work.

Beyond the basic need of Christian conversion, every person has at least three broad needs to which his church's program of teaching must be effectively geared.

The first of these is *a continuously vital relationship to Jesus Christ.* This outcome is not automatic. Sometimes Christian workers wonder why certain individuals who have joined the church become indifferent to their Christian responsibilities and lapse into careless and unworthy conduct. In many instances the failure lies with the church's educational ministry. It fails to teach and train these persons in such a way as to help them remain faithful to the Lord and to his church.

A second need is for *a Christian interpretation of life.* The mere fact that an individual has made a profession of faith does not guarantee that he will approach the totality of life from a Christian perspective. He must be taught to think Christ's thoughts after him. He must continually be transformed by the renewing of his mind.

A third need is for *a growing Christian experience.* Actually, if the second need is met, much has already been done to insure the meeting of this need. But here, too, Christian education has a vital role to play. Without help from their churches, very few Christians develop beyond the stage of spiritual babyhood.

Families must also be helped by the church's educational ministry. To lead persons to understand, appreciate, and accept the Christian view of the home is one of the most needed ministries of our day. Teaching children and youth the ideals of Christian marriage must begin early and be faithfully continued. Prevention of unfortunate marriages by preparing young people for good marriages is a far better strategy than trying to remedy bad marital situations after they have developed.

Furthermore, families that are already established must be helped to see that to the home belongs the primary responsibility for the moral and spiritual teaching of children. This in no sense rules out the church's educational work, for families must be given wise assistance in the teaching and training of their boys and girls. If the home is to fulfill its God-given mission, the church will not say, "Send us your children that we may teach them"; rather, it will say, "God has given you the duty of teaching your children; we are available and ready to help you do this in the best possible way."

The Current Situation Requires It

Moral, social, and spiritual conditions in today's world urgently call for vitalized programs of Christian teaching and training. These programs must be relevant to contemporary needs. Unless church curriculums become more effective in drawing people to Christ and making church members more thoroughly Christian, it is only a question of time until the church will have lost a great measure of its influence in the modern world. In fact, that influence is already in serious decline.

Spiritual illiteracy abounds. One confirmation of the fact is the poor showing made on tests of Bible knowledge given to various groups of people of various ages. The results indicate a low literacy level not only on the part of the general populace but of church members as well.

A moral revolution is taking place. Old established values are being discarded by many people. This revolution is affecting not only unbelievers but also church members. It has become common for many church people to follow the practices of the non-Christian segment of society rather than to live as the New Testament teaches.

We face staggering social problems. Race relations continues to be one of them. Churches have the tremendous responsibility of leading people to take seriously Christ's teachings as to the worth of every human personality. Professing Christians must learn to put Christlike love into practice in all human relationships.

The world is growing more pagan every day. Secularism and materialism are being exalted above spirituality. Sinister forces threaten all of the values Christianity stands for. The church has become so greatly affected by the world that in many cases the major flow of influence is from the world to the church rather than from the church to the world.

Modern scientific advances have precipitated a tremendous technological revolution. This revolution threatens to rule God, Christ, and the church out of all consideration in the thinking of some. Can God still be meaningful to persons in such an age as this? Can Christ yet mold our modern world? Is the Bible now to be regarded as an outmoded piece of writing with no significant message for today's needs?

Earnest Christians desire with all their hearts that God and spiritual values shall become increasingly meaningful to people everywhere. But if the Christian answer is to become real in the experience of today's people, the church has on its hands a stupendous task of Christian education.

Christian education will not immediately solve all of our problems, but the conditions we face in today's world demand the best that ministers and leaders of churches and denominations can do to provide genuine Christian teaching and training for as many persons as can possibly be reached.

Some may reply that what we really need is a fresh outpouring of the Holy Spirit that will bring people to conviction of sin and repentance. With that sentiment we are thoroughly agreed, but the kind of Christian education we envision in this book is permeated and controlled by the power of the Spirit. Otherwise it is not worthy of being called Christian. Spiritual renewal and Christian teaching must go hand in hand. Each must help the other, and each *will* help the other if each is genuine.

Who, Then, Shall Be Taught?

A church must teach every person it can possibly reach.

With some churches, outreach efforts are almost nonexistent. These churches seem satisfied just to teach the children of their own families, and for the most part any additions to their membership come only from those families. The picture thus presented is largely that of a self-satisfied, self-contained, inbred group of the faithful (?) who have neither the vision nor the compassion to go outside of their own limited circle to reach and teach others for whom Christ died.

Persons of every age group, *including adults,* need Christian education. One of the strong points of the educational programs of *some* American Protestant denominations has been the emphasis on reaching and teaching adults. There are indications, however, that such work is slackening in some areas. It would be a great tragedy if American churches ever came to the point where many European churches have always been, simply aiming the ministry of religious education at boys and girls and ignoring the needs of adults.

Furthermore, the intergenerational aspect of the church's teaching ministry must not be overlooked. Of course, the church should continue to teach age-graded groups; but there is also a need and a place for teaching the community of faith as a total group. All persons in the church's life above the age of early childhood should be the objects of such education collectively. More about this will be found at the close of chapter 4.

Who Teaches?

D. Campbell Wyckoff has pointed out that in Christian education there is a profound sense in which God himself is the teacher. That accords with Jesus' reference to the Holy Spirit as a teacher who guides his disciples "into all truth" (John 14:26; 16:13). As we have noted earlier, Jesus was himself the Master Teacher. So it is correct to say that in Christian teaching, the triune God—Father, Son, and Holy Spirit—is the supreme teacher. But further, as Dr. Wyckoff observes, "it is not just his message, but his active and moving presence, that figures in the educational transaction. This changes the relations and roles of teacher and learner rather profoundly."[1] As Christian believers we accept that significant fact. And we rejoice in such a challenging and encouraging reality as foundational to our God-given task.

We move on to recognize that Christian education is a function of the church as a whole. It is not the responsibility of just a few of the members, but of all.

The entire church must be the agency through which God communicates with the world. The church's educational work is so important that no Christian can escape the burden of it.

In an inescapable sense, every Christian is called upon to be a teacher—if not in a formal, institutional way, certainly in reality. This is true because again and again a church's best opportunity to bear its witness to the unbelieving world comes in those incidental situations in everyday life when the individual Christian must speak and act in support of his faith. Therefore, even church members who are neither parents nor educational workers in the church's organized life have a responsibility to teach the Christian faith to the world.

Furthermore, all members of a church make up the Christian community which influences the lives and attitudes of developing persons—children, youth, and adults. The only way the Christian faith can become relevant and credible to the younger generation and to persons outside the church is for them to see it operative in the lives of church members.

For all of these reasons, every member is inescapably involved in the work of Christian teaching, for he is part of a fellowship which is constantly teaching, both by what it says and by what it is and does.

The facts this chapter has presented lead us to these conclusions: (1) Christian education is still valid and still needed. (2) Any neglect by a church of its teaching responsibility is serious. (3) The work demands a much greater expenditure of time, thought, and effort than is presently the practice in many places. (4) There are no easy solutions to the problems of Christian education. (5) The work is worthy of our best efforts.

In fulfilling its educational ministry, a church needs a strong organizational base and a sound curriculum. The rest of this book will deal with these matters, particularly the theory and design of curriculum. An understanding of your church's curriculum is essential to your most effective work in Christian education.

Note

1. The quotation is from a personal letter from Dr. Wyckoff to the authors.

2
Revolution in Christian Education

The word *revolution,* to many people, conjures up the thought of radicals taking over a foreign government. Although the word is used accurately when describing a *coup d'etat,* it also has many other meanings.

A *revolution,* according to Webster, is a "complete or radical change of any kind." During recent decades, radical changes have taken place in the curriculum designs and resource materials prepared for use in almost all of the churches in the United States and Canada. These new designs and resources, in turn, are stimulating and helping to sustain significant changes in the educational ministries of churches. As a result, future historians may describe the latter part of the twentieth century as the most eventful period in the history of Christian education in modern times.

Forces Which Influenced Changes

Several forces in American life during the decades following World War II influenced these major changes. To understand the new curriculum designs and resource materials, one must understand some of the forces which produced them. Four forces have been especially influential. They are (1) a revival of interest in Christianity and the church, (2) a resurgence of concern for theological realities, (3) dramatic advances in education, and (4) the emergence of new life-styles in America.

1. *Revival of Interest in Christianity and the Church*

At the close of World War II, the American people were frustrated and emotionally exhausted. Approximately 300,000 American youth had been killed in one of the most costly wars in history. Thousands of others were left physically maimed for life. Moral and psychological problems left permanent scars in the lives of thousands of additional persons. Hardly any community escaped at least one serious casualty of the horrors of war.

Added to this frustration and emotional exhaustion was a sense of moral perplexity. The horrors of war had seemed to push to the limit man's inhumanity to man. The inhuman torture and massacre of over six million Jews in Germany had caused the American people to protest in righteous indignation. The excruciating pain and wholesale death resulting from the dropping of atomic bombs in Japan forced on thoughtful people all over America feelings of pity and a gnawing fear that the end might not have justified the means.

Out of this frustration, emotional exhaustion, and moral perplexity came a resurgence of interest in Christianity and the church. Old value systems had failed and people were left spiritually destitute. Scores of people, heretofore only nominally interested, if at all, in Christianity, turned to the church and the Christian faith for strength, for answers to perplexing questions, and for a sense of the meaning of life.

The needs and concerns of the American people during these postwar years led to a reappraisal of church curriculum materials. In the light of the needs and concerns of the day, the curriculum materials were tested and many of them were found wanting. Thoughtful church and denominational leaders recognized a need for a complete reorganization of curriculum designs and the development of materials which would help to communicate the relevance of the Christian faith to the contemporary needs and concerns of people.

2. *Resurgence of Concern for Theological Realities*

During the latter part of the nineteenth century and the early part of the twentieth century a liberal theology enjoyed wide popularity throughout the country. Although conservative groups were strong in some sections, a majority of the nationally known theologians were liberals. Consequently, the prevailing theological atmosphere was liberal. The doctrine of the transcendence of God was eclipsed by a strong emphasis on his immanence. The natural goodness of man and his ability to grow into the kingdom were widely accepted doctrines. The accompanying social gospel emphasized the fruits of the Christian faith but gave little attention to its roots.

The spiritual destitution resulting from experiences of World War II accelerated a theological movement already under way in this country and in Europe. This movement magnified the transcendence of God, the divinity and redemptive mission of Christ, the sinfulness of man, salvation by grace, and the meaning of Christian discipleship.

This resurgence of concern for the great realities of the Christian faith exerted profound influence upon the leading Christian educators of the post World War II period. The religious education movement, strong from the turn of the century to the beginning of World War II, had placed major emphasis on Christian nurture, social experience, and divine immanence. Leaders of the movement, such as George Albert Coe, Harrison Elliott, and Ernest Chave, although outstanding educators, had reflected the liberal theology of their day.

Sheldon Smith, in his *Faith and Nurture,*[1] vigorously attacked the theological assumptions of the religious education movement. With the essential doctrines of the Christian faith as criteria, he demonstrated point by point the incompatibility of the theological tenets of the religious education movement with anything that has ever been recognized by the church in the past as normative Christianity.

James D. Smart appealed to Christian educators to recognize as the purpose of education in the church to continue the work of Jesus and the early church. From a study of its biblical beginnings, Smart asserted that the educational goal of the church is to "teach so that through our teaching God may work in the hearts of those whom we teach to make of them disciples wholly committed to his gospel, with an understanding of it, and with a personal faith that will enable them to bear convincing witness to it in word and action in the midst of an unbelieving world."[2]

Randolph Crump Miller asserted that theology is the clue to Christian education. He challenged leaders in Christian education to seek a

> rediscovery of a relevant theology which will bridge the gap between content and method, providing the background and perspective of Christian truth by which the best methods and content will be used as tools to bring the learners into the right relationship with the living God who is revealed to us in Jesus Christ, using the guidance of parents and the fellowship of life in the Church as environments in which Christian nurture will take place.[3]

David Hunter stated that most education in the church is not based on personal encounter with God but, rather on instruction, on teaching about someone else's encounter. Personal encounter with God, Hunter affirmed, is the very essence of Christian education. This encounter Hunter calls engagement.[4]

This shift of emphasis from the humanistic concerns of the religious education movement during prewar years forced a reevaluation of curriculum designs and resource materials used in the churches. In many cases, it was found that the new wine could not be put into the old wineskins. Completely new designs and resource materials were needed. Even evangelical denominations which had not been influenced significantly by liberal theology experienced an increasing concern for the biblical and theological content in their curriculums. This led them to seek new ways to communicate the mighty acts of God through printed pages.

3. *Dramatic Advances in Public Education*

The years since World War II have witnessed dramatic advances in public education. Former Commissioner of Education James E. Allen said of this period:

> Never before in history have our schools engaged in such widespread experimentation to meet the new educational requirement. Never before have so many hopeful new approaches been developed in such a relatively short period. An intense self-examination is now under way on a national scale. In the process we are learning that many of the old ways of operating our schools are not necessarily the best ways.[5]

Spawning these changes in public education has been a proliferation of curriculum studies. Throughout the country there have been multitudinous studies of almost all aspects of public education. These studies have been conducted by local school systems, state boards of education, professional groups, university centers, and other groups of concerned educators.

Results of these curriculum studies have influenced life in schools all over America. Some of the innovations are in the content of study. The new mathematics, for example, is a radically new concept for teaching one of the oldest subjects in the curriculum. Although perhaps less dramatic, innovations also have taken place in approaches to teaching physics, chemistry, foreign languages, and other familiar subjects.

Public education curriculum studies also have led to dramatic advances in school organization and in instructional methods. In many schools, the traditional lockstep system of moving students up through successive grades has given way to an ungraded or to a broadly graded system.

Electronic media are making an impact on classroom teaching. Educational television is bringing to millions of students courses carefully prepared and taught by highly trained specialists. Whereas educational TV is geared to mass education, another electronic marvel, the computer, is being hailed as the ultimate in individualized instruction. Through computer-assisted instruction, the individual student is able to progress through a course at his own speed in keeping with his ability and temperament.

Since the early sixties, there also has been tremendous upsurge of interest in adult education. The rapid acceleration of change has forced thoughtful people to realize that a person, during childhood and youth, cannot acquire and store up all of the knowledge and skills which he or she will need throughout adulthood. Millions of adults have returned to school, or enrolled in other forms of education, to acquire new understandings and skills. By 1980, the adult education movement had become one of the largest and most rapidly growing movements in America.

This general ferment in public education has been a stimulant to Christian educators. They believe that the uniqueness of the content of their curriculums is a challenge to discover and utilize the best principles and methods available for involving persons in learning experiences which will stimulate growth toward the objectives of Christian education.

4. *Emergence of New Life-styles*

Dramatic changes in the life-styles of millions of Americans also have had a major impact on the development of curriculum plans and resource materials. Thoughtful Christian educators have been forced to explore the relevance of the Christian gospel to persons who have made deliberate choices of new life-styles and, also, for persons whose life-styles have been shaped or changed by circumstances over which seemingly they have little or no control.

Impatience or frustration with "the establishment" caused thousands of youth and young adults, especially during the sixties and early seventies, to search for innovative ways to cope with the perplexities of life. Some joined the hippies, or similar movements. Essentially this represented a withdrawal from "the system." Others joined activist groups committed to changing "the system," by violence if necessary.

During more recent years, these subcultures and activist movements have not attracted as many youth to life-styles completely alien to the life-styles of their parents, but their ideologies are continuing to influence thousands of youth and young adults of the eighties. These youth and young adults may not live in communes, or seize presidents' offices on college campuses, but their rebellion against traditional ideals and established customs expresses itself in more subtle ways. How is the Christian gospel relevant to the legitimate concerns which caused these youth and young adults deliberately to choose new life-styles and value systems? How can churches, through outreach and Christian education, reach and minister to these persons? These are some of the problems which have forced, and continue to force, religious educators to restudy curriculum designs and resource materials recommended for use in churches.

Changes in family patterns also have forced religious educators to reassess curriculum designs and resource materials and to revise some approaches. The increasing prevalence of the single-parent family and the practice of cohabitation without matrimony are only two phenomena which demand attention in Christian education.

During the eighties, high inflation and a major energy crisis are forcing changes in the life-styles of millions of individuals. Churches and denominational agencies also are being forced to change traditional ways of operation to cope with these forces over which they seemingly have no control. All of this is forcing thought about how Christian education can best be planned and conducted in churches all over America.

Studies Which Produced Change

These and other forces in American life since World War II have stimulated tremendous activity among persons responsible for developing and publishing denominational curriculum designs and resource materials. Most of the denominations have engaged in major curriculum studies. These studies have included a careful reexamination of the fundamental objectives of Christian education and a search for the most effective designs for achieving those objectives. To understand the new materials which have been and are being introduced in American churches, one needs to have some understanding of the curriculum studies and the resulting designs which produced these materials.

The Cooperative Curriculum Project

One of the first of these studies was the Cooperative Curriculum Project. This four-year study (1960-64) was conducted by more than one hundred curriculum specialists from sixteen denominations. In the study, participants addressed themselves to the basic question, "What kind of curriculum is needed by our churches in the task of Christian education?"

It was not the purpose of this interdenominational study to develop specific curriculum plans and materials. Participants agreed from the beginning that the development of materials is the task of denominations working individually or in clusters.

The principal objective of the project was to explore the major elements which should go into a basic design for curriculum materials. Elements included in the study were objectives, scope, context, learning tasks, curriculum areas, themes, and an organizing principle. Although the various denominations might state these differently in terms of their respective doctrines and polity, these are the kinds of elements, the participants concluded, which should go into a curriculum base design.

These elements in a curriculum design are defined in chapters 3 and 4. A complete report of the Cooperative Curriculum Project appears in *The Church's Educational Ministry: A Curriculum Plan.*[6]

Denominations participating in the Cooperative Curriculum Project did so for the purpose of enriching their own respective curriculums. Although a few of the participating denominations continued to work together in producing materials, most of them have used insights gained from the project in developing their own individual curriculum designs and materials.

Christian Education: Shared Approaches

In 1967 another cooperative curriculum movement emerged in American Protestantism. Although not a direct outgrowth of the Cooperative Curriculum Project (CCP), it did (and does) utilize and further project many of the philosophical concepts and educational strategies prominent in CCP. Some of the denominations which participated in CCP regrouped to give leadership to this new movement.

The name of the new movement was Joint Educational Development (JED). Its founders were the Episcopal Church, the United Church of Christ, and the United Presbyterian Church in the U.S.A. Later these three denominations were joined by the Christian Church (Disciples of Christ), Church of the Brethren, Cumberland Presbyterian Church, Evangelical Covenant Church, Moravian Church in America, Presbyterian Church in Canada, Presbyterian Church in the U.S., Reformed Church in America, and the United Church of Canada.

One of the most successful projects of JED is Christian Education: Shared

Approaches (CE:SA). Introduced in phases from the fall of 1975 through the fall of 1978, it has been adopted by eleven of the twelve denominations in JED. A few other denominations, including the American Baptist Churches and The United Methodist Church, participate in parts of CE:SA.

As did CCP, CE:SA seeks to break the traditional concept that printed materials alone comprise the curriculum. Whereas CCP attacked the traditional concept by expanding the concept of curriculum, CE:SA's primary emphasis is on the interrelationship of printed resources and other components in the church's educational program. CE:SA conceives the church's educational program as a unified system of interdependent components. Components in the system are (1) theological and educational affirmations, (2) teaching and learning opportunities, (3) leader development and support, (4) curriculum resources, and (5) planning and evaluation.

John J. Spangler, JED's planning and program coordinator, says that "the major emphasis of CE:SA is upon *interdependence, integrity, harmony,* and *coordination* of all the components so education can contribute to the fulfillment of the mission of the church."[7]

Overall directions, purposes, and intentions of educational ministry are outlined in the statements which follow.[8] These statements, which have been adopted by JED, undergird four basic approaches utilized in CE:SA for stimulating and guiding learning experiences in Christian education.

> 1. The Christian community engages in education as a continuing means of sharing the gospel and of helping persons to make their own responses of faith; to broaden and deepen their perceptions of God, other persons, social issues and structures, and the natural world; and to develop skills of ethical decision-making and responsible participation in shaping the future of the human community.

> 2. The Christian community engages in education as a means of equipping persons to understand, to enter into, and to help develop the life and ministries of a contemporary community of faith, rooted in the Christian heritage and charged with mission.

> 3. The Christian community engages in education as a means for helping persons to achieve the full human stature that we believe God intends. This involves:

> a. a sense of personal dignity, capacity, and worth;
> b. interpersonal relationships of trust, freedom, and love;

c. a global society that enhances freedom, justice, and
   peace for all people.

4. The Christian community engages in education as a means of
effecting justice and reconciliation within and through all social
structures and systems. Essential to accomplishing this intention
is an understanding of the interdependence of all people and a
willingness to act to change the present unjust distribution of
power and economic resources in the world.

Sharing is a key idea in the CE:SA plan. Sharing takes place in three special
areas.

1. *Shared approaches*

The denominations participating in CE:SA recognize four basic approaches
for involvement in Christian education. Each of these approaches provides a
wide range of possibilities for planning, guiding, and being involved in learning experiences in Christian education. Churches may choose one of the four
or mix and match all four.

The four approaches are (1) knowing the Word, (2) interpreting the Word, (3)
living the Word, and (4) doing the Word.

The goal of "knowing the Word" is to enable persons to know the *contents*
of the Bible and to respond as faithful disciples. The primary constituency of
this approach includes persons who feel that understanding the Bible is the
major task of Christian education. Learning opportunities are offered in a
weekly church school setting in which dated materials are used.

The goal of "interpreting the Word" is "to increase the ability of the people
of God to respond to the Scriptures, equipping them to be responsible interpreters of Scriptures."[9] The primary constituency includes persons who
desire a disciplined, critical study of the Bible. Learning opportunities are
offered in settings ranging from church school sessions to retreats.

The goal of "living the Word" is "to enable persons to participate in the life
of the Christian community and its mission in the world as disciples of Jesus
Christ, Lord, and Savior."[10] The primary constituency includes persons who
desire to relate the Christian heritage to life. Learning opportunities are
offered in a wide range of groupings and settings in the congregation.

The goal of "doing the Word" is to "enable persons to become increasingly
committed to, equipped for, and experienced in participating in God's mission
for the world, and to know both the joy and the cost of faithfulness in this mis-

sion."[11] The primary constituency includes persons who recognize a corporate and individual mission response. Learning opportunities are offered in a broad range of settings, including a strong intergenerational emphasis.

2. *Shared responsibility*

Denominations involved in CE:SA also share responsibility in the planning and conducting of Christian education in their churches. Denominational leaders and agencies share with one another in developing designs and planning and producing resource materials. Further sharing takes place between denominational agencies and individual congregations within the denomination. Although agencies prepare resources and suggest designs, congregational leaders are invited "to determine the needs and concerns of life as expressed by its members. Once these needs and concerns are determined, the local 'approach' should be developed by leaders in the congregation."[12] Major resources are described below.

3. *Shared resources*

The basic printed resources in CE:SA is an annual publication entitled *General Prospectus, Christian Education: Shared Approaches.* It describes material resources prepared for use in the congregations of the fourteen denominations participating in the plan. For each of the four approaches described in the preceding section, the prospectus describes possible (1) goals, (2) teaching/learning opportunities, (3) suggestions for leader development and support, (4) helps for planning and evaluation, and (5) descriptions of available material resources.

Material resources described in the prospectus include publications and other resources available for use with the various age groups (or intergenerational groups) in pursuing each of the four approaches.

For additional information on CE:SA, see Appendix B (pp. 153-158).

Denominational Studies

Influenced, in varying degrees, by the Cooperative Curriculum Project, three major denominations in America have conducted largely independent studies and developed their curriculum plans and resources.

1. *Lutheran Church in America*

Luther Lindberg, LCA's director of curriculum planning for the eighties, says:

Planning for Educational Ministry in the Parish began for the LCA in the early 1970's on the heels of its Parish Education Curriculum program of the 1960's. Educational ministry in the LCA continues to be concerned with growth and change in persons. It is seen as a continually developing process that is shaped and reshaped to meet the needs of Christian persons and groups as they mature in Christ. Therefore, what is happening in the congregations of the church in the 1980's is not seen as a sharp break with past efforts but rather as a process of building on the foundations which are proven by time and experience. Among the foundations which give shape to the ongoing educational ministry efforts of the church are the following: a monumental research effort on the process of Christian growth *(How Persons Grow in Christian Community,* 1973); a concept of partnership involving congregations, their synods, and the church at large; a carefully developed Central Objective plus a detailed series of age level objectives; the understanding that education is not identical with learning (learning goes on continually in almost every situation in which Christian persons find themselves; education is planned learning); the belief that attitudes can indeed be modified through experience; the understanding that by virtue of growing up in society persons inevitably become involved in certain "continual life involvements" which may be seen in Christian perspective and which serve as significant take-hold points for learning. Certain practical implications emerge from these viewpoints:

1. Learners are likely to be genuinely interested because they are being reached at levels of real concerns.

2. Integration of the educational process takes place within the learner and not in some external curriculum. In other words, the learners are the integrators. They change because the new experiences have meaning and are relevant to them.

3. The fact that key involvements are common to everyone makes it possible to design education for groups and not solely on an individual basis.

The goal of educational ministry, therefore, is stated as follows:

The central objective for educational ministry in the Lutheran Church in America shall be to assist persons—

to perceive, respond to, and participate in God's continuing activity and revelation, particularly in Jesus Christ, in the human and Christian communities as they deal with their continual life involvements of—
being a person,
relating to persons and groups, and
living in society, culture, and the physical universe.

The process has eventuated in the development of a resource bank of curriculum units from which congregations may tailor-make their own programs. Considerable guidance is provided by the church and synods in the selection of parish programs which are not only directly related to local needs but which are educationally sound in reflecting the faith of the church in its biblical, theological, and contemporary dimensions.

Efforts are underway at the present time to fashion the next generation of educational ministry viewpoints and resources which build on the shoulders of the efforts mentioned above.[13]

2. *The United Methodist Church*

John P. Gilbert, of the Curriculum Resource Committee of the United Methodist Church, says:

In 1968, The Methodist Church and The Evangelical United Brethren Church united and became The United Methodist Church. The new church adopted the curriculum plan which had been developed jointly by the former Methodist Church and the Evangelical United Brethren during the years since 1960.

In 1979, the church published a statement, *Foundations for Teaching and Learning in The United Methodist Church,* which sought to identify the denomination's theology and philosophy of religious education. This statement replaced a similar document originally published in 1960 and based on the work of the Cooperative Curriculum Project.

The 1979 statement identifies the goal of Christian education in this way: The fundamental goal of Christian education is the development of Christian faith and discipleship. This goal is broken into several parts that help in understanding the goal. These parts or aims are both means and ends. They are the means of accomplishing the goal and because they are parts of the overall goal they express the utimate intentions of the enterprise of Christian education in the church. The ten aims, identified through the denomination's faith statement, are these:

> To enlarge our grasp of the Bible
> To commune with God
> To appropriate and renew our tradition
> To receive God's grace and grow in faith
> To take up our ministry
> To take part in the church's nurture and mission
> To make ethical decisions
> To serve as stewards of God's gifts
> To work toward common goals
> To communicate our faith.

Curriculum resources published by The United Methodist Church still are based largely on the work of the Cooperative Curriculum Project. But the denomination's curriculum developers are presently deeply engaged in evaluating the currency of the

Cooperative Curriculum Project approach for the last decades of the twentieth century.

Special attention is being paid to insights from new learning theories and in the areas of cognitive, moral, and faith development. The means of integrating the rich ethnic and cultural traditions of members of The United Methodist Church and its predecessor bodies into the church while at the same time affirming those special traditions also occupies the attention of curriculum developers. And the task of helping each person to become directly engaged in the theological task, thereby affirming the theological diversity and pluralism of The United Methodist Church is of special concern. Curriculum developers strive to understand the ways in which the curriculum and its resources can speak directly to these concerns.

While steps in the development of new concepts of curriculum for the church are being considered, the denomination continues to publish Bible-based curriculum resources for children, youth, and adults. As in the past, the use of options, choices, and alternatives among the various resources or within the resources is a hallmark of The United Methodist curriculum.[14]

3. *Southern Baptists*

The educational program in Southern Baptist churches is conducted through five program organizations. They are the Sunday School, Church Training, Woman's Missionary Union, Brotherhood, and Music Ministry.

Representative leaders of those program organizations worked together during the latter part of the sixties in developing a correlated church curriculum design. Two of those representative leaders had participated in the four-year Cooperative Curriculum Project; through them, many of the educational insights and principles of CCP influenced the development of the new Southern Baptist Curriculum design. (See Appendix A.)

The purpose of the new curriculum design was to make available a correlated curriculum providing appropriately for implementing the teaching-training tasks for a church. Curriculum materials implementing the new correlated curriculum were introduced in the churches in 1970.

Ten years later, as these lines are being written, leaders of the same program organizations are involved in an update of the Church Curriculum Base Design. The update is scheduled for completion in 1984.

It is anticipated that the Curriculum Base Design Update will continue to organize the curriculum plan around certain key elements. Three of the foundational elements are:

1. An overarching objective, or statement of mission, of a church.

2. Four functions, or statements of intention, designed to lead a church to do its work in ways consistent with its nature and mission. (These functions are to *worship,* to *proclaim and witness,* to *nurture and educate,* and to *minister.)*

3. Church tasks which define the continuing activities performed by a church to carry out its functions and accomplish its mission. (These tasks are assigned to the educational organizations for programming. The major task of the Sunday School, for example, is to teach the Bible. Church Training is responsible for equipping church members for discipleship and personal ministry. Involved in this task is teaching Christian theology and Baptist doctrine, Christian ethics, Christian history, and church polity and organization. The task of the Music Ministry is to develop musical skills, attitudes, and understandings. The Woman's Missionary Union and Brotherhood involve persons in the study and practice of Christian missions.)

The Church Curriculum Base Design also includes principles and guidelines which each program organization uses in further developing curriculum plans and general and age-level resources to implement its assigned tasks.

For additional information on this curriculum design, see illustrations used in chapters 3 and 4 and, also, Appendix A.

Elements Which Reflect Change

Many new curriculum designs and materials have come into existence as a result of these denominational studies. Although different in many ways, most of them have at least three things in common.

1. Their Objectives Are Theological

In sharp contrast with many church curriculum plans in vogue earlier, most of the curriculum designs and resources developed since 1960 have clearly stated theological objectives.

This feature is illustrated in the objectives cited in the preceding section. A review of these objectives will reveal that most of them are developed around two basic ideas: revelation and response. The revelatory element is expressed in The United Methodist curriculum objective: "to help persons become aware of God's seeking love as shown especially in Jesus Christ." The desired response is stated equally clearly: "to respond in faith and love to the end that . . ."; and the last part of the objective contains a description of specific ways the Christian's response to revelation should be expressed.

Objectives of many other curriculums reveal as the ultimate purpose helping persons experience God's love and saving power and to live daily as devoted Christian disciples in contemporary society.

2. *The Approach Is Holistic*

Fragmentation characterized educational programs in many churches prior to World War II. The various educational organizations—Sunday School, the missionary organizations, the Sunday evening training program, and others—each had its own program and curriculum. Any correlation existing in these multiple programs and curriculums often was accidental.

The picture was further complicated by occasional efforts of denominational agencies whose functions were not primarily educational to secure time and promotion in the church educational organizations. A board of evangelism, for example, might make a direct approach to the Sunday School leaders in local churches. Consequently, the failure of the Board of Christian Education and the Board of Evangelism to coordinate their work on a denominational level created confusion in the churches they were established to serve.

The curriculum studies of several denominations have corrected both of these problems. Representatives of all denominational agencies having a direct ministry in the churches have participated in one way or another in the studies. As a result, their concerns have been built into the curriculum designs in such a way that curriculum materials carry units undergirding the total educational ministry of the church, including its relationship to all denominational agencies.

Moreover, designs growing out of the studies have encompassed the total educational ministry of the church. The work of all program organizations has been properly coordinated in a comprehensive plan for achieving the ultimate educational objective of the church.

3. *Their Function Is Church Oriented*

The Sunday School movement came into existence outside of churches and its acceptance in churches was a slow and, at times, painful experience. This was the experience also of numerous other educational organizations in the churches of various denominations. Although they had gained acceptance in the churches generally before World War II, there continued to be the feeling on the part of many people that the Sunday School and other program organizations were sponsored by the church, housed in the church, but not integral parts of the church itself.

One important factor which led to the curriculum studies was the growing conviction of many church leaders that the church itself has a basic education function. This conviction was stated most clearly by James D. Smart when he said, "The church must teach, just as it must preach, or it will not be the church. Responsibility rests on the whole church even though certain workers undertake specific assignments."[15]

The curriculum designs and materials growing out of the denominational curriculum studies make clear the fact that the educational organizations of a church are not appendages to the church. They are expressions of the church's basic nature.

The Presbyterian Church in the U.S., in stating the premise on which its Covenant Life Curriculum was founded, described this prevailing concept of the role of Christian education in churches. "The church educates," affirmed the Presbyterians, "by drawing people into its own life as it lives in covenant with God and bears witness to the Word of God."[16]

Notes

1. (New York: Charles Scribner's Son, 1941).

2. *The Teaching Ministry of the Church* (Philadelphia: The Westminster Press, 1954), p. 107.

3. *The Clue to Christian Education* (New York: Charles Scribner's Sons, 1950), p. 15.

4. *Christian Education as Engagement* (New York: Seabury Press, 1963), p. 7.

5. In Arthur D. Morse, *Schools of Tomorrow—Today* (Garden City: Doubleday & Co., 1960), p. 6.

6. *The Church's Educational Ministry: A Curriculum Plan* (St. Louis: The Bethany Press, 1965).

7. Statement in personal letter, dated April 18, 1980, from John J. Spangler.

8. *DOING CHURCH EDUCATION TOGETHER: Why and How JED Works* (Atlanta: John Knox Press, 1978), p. 7. Used by permission.

9. Arthur O. Van Eck, *Learning for Discipleship* (Atlanta: Presbyterian Church in the U.S., 1978), p. 69.

10. Ibid.

11. Ibid., p. 70.

12. *General Prospectus, Christian Education: Shared Approaches,* 1980-81 edition, p. 3.

13. The authors express appreciation to Dr. Lindberg for preparing this description of the LCA curriculum design for publication in this book.

14. The authors express appreciation to Dr. Gilbert for preparing this description of the curriculum design of The United Methodist Church for publication in this book.

15. Smart, *Teaching Ministry,* p. 11.

16. Sue Nichols, "The Covenant Life Curriculum," *International Journal of Religious Education,* November, 1964, pp. 8-9.

3
Curriculum Design:
From Objectives to Organizing Principle

In order to understand and appreciate your church's curriculum, it is important to know something about the principles on which it is built. A good curriculum is based on a sound curriculum philosophy and a worthy curriculum plan.

A curriculum is something like a tree. A tree's trunk, branches, and leaves are only a part of its total system. The extensive but invisible root system which is below the ground is so essential to its life that without it the tree could not exist. It is similar with a curriculum. Though its roots may not be obvious to everyone, they are in many respects the most important part. A curriculum's root system includes theological insights, educational philosophy, and a plan technically referred to as curriculum design. The drawing on page 42 illustrates the relation of these parts of curriculum.

Some persons are hardly aware of that which lies behind the curriculum of their church. They would be surprised to learn the details of the long, painstaking process required to plan it.

A highly trained corps of workers cooperates in the task. This calls for hard work, thorough knowledge of theological and educational principles, and skill in the application of those principles. Without such knowledge, labor, and skill there could be no worthy teaching materials such as quarterlies, study course books, pictures, and flipcharts. The educational program of the average church would be seriously handicapped if it lacked such helps.

In this chapter and the next we shall discuss basic elements of curriculum theory and design. Some of these have been recognized and applied by curriculum planners for a long time. Others, however, represent fairly recent insights growing out of the studies referred to in the previous chapter. In some instances these newer insights give us the clue to significant curriculum improvements. They are now being used advantageously by the staffs of most of the denominational publishing houses.

What Is Curriculum?

The term "curriculum" is from the Latin. It is a noun derived from the verb *currere,* which means to run. Literally, a curriculum is a running or a race course.

The common conception of curriculum is that it is a course of study in an educational institution—or the whole body of courses offered by such an institution. With reference to church curriculum, the usual idea is that it means the total program of teaching and training. However, many persons probably think of their church's curriculum as consisting of the printed resources such as quarterlies and books.

A sounder concept is now quite generally held by curriculum planners. That concept is that curriculum exists only where true learning experiences take place. Accordingly, a church's curriculum may be thought of as the sum of all learning experiences resulting from a curriculum plan used under church guidance and directed toward achieving a church's objective.

This means that the denominational publishing house does not provide the curriculum! The curriculum is what happens to the learner in the local situation. The publisher only furnishes a curriculum plan and curriculum materials. We must not confuse the curriculum plan with the curriculum, for they are not the same. The curriculum plan is embodied in the printed materials and resources, whereas the curriculum is what occurs in the teaching-learning situation.

Throughout this volume, we shall use the word *curriculum* to denote the sum total of learning experiences in the local situation.

How Is Curriculum Related to Program?

Essential to a sound understanding of a church's curriculum is an awareness of the relation the curriculum bears to the church's total program. This relation is depicted in the drawing on page 41. By referring to that drawing as you read the next several paragraphs, you should be able to get an accurate concept.

A church's program is broader than its curriculum. "Program" is the overarching, umbrella term; "church program" refers to the sum of all the activities a church engages in as it moves toward achieving its mission. Church program in this sense includes (1) curriculum and (2) performance activities.

By performance activities we mean congregational, organizational, and

CHURCH PROGRAM

1. Curriculum
   (learning experiences)

2. Performance Activities
   (performing the functions
   of the church)

   ● Worship

   ● Proclamation and Witness

   ● Nurture and Education

   ● Ministry

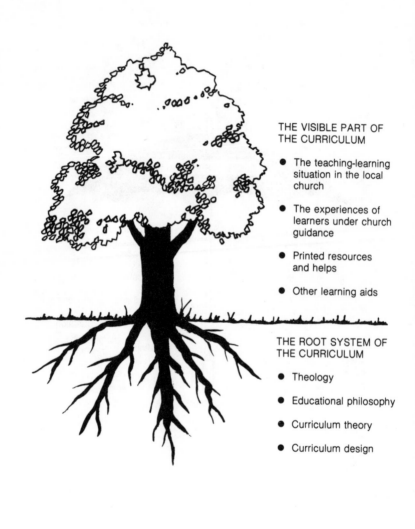

THE VISIBLE PART OF
THE CURRICULUM

- The teaching-learning
  situation in the local
  church

- The experiences of
  learners under church
  guidance

- Printed resources
  and helps

- Other learning aids

THE ROOT SYSTEM OF
THE CURRICULUM

- Theology

- Educational philosophy

- Curriculum theory

- Curriculum design

cational objective, as stated by designers of Southern Baptist cur-
terials, reads as follows:

lp persons become aware of God as revealed in Scripture and most fully in Jesus
respond to him in a personal commitment of faith, strive to follow him in the full
of discipleship, relate effectively to his church and its mission in the world, live
ious recognition of the guidance and power of the Holy Spirit, and grow toward
maturity.

ve is used as a tool for curriculum planning and evaluation. The
nat curriculum content, methods, learning goals, and specific
ld be in harmony with this curriculum purpose.

What Does Curriculum Include?

name for what we are here considering is *scope.* One of the
tions of *scope* is "the range within which an activity displays
e of curriculum is that which is appropriate to be dealt with in
t is more than subject matter. It includes subject matter, of
ly means *subject matter in relation to experience.*
Christian education curriculum, rightly considered, has the
. Actually, so important is the Bible in the church's educa-
t chapter 8 of this volume is completely devoted to it. Some
o turn to that chapter before proceeding further in this one.
le is the basis and starting point of all Christian education
as defined, is everything that is appropriate to be dealt with
his means that the scope is not only as broad as the gospel
an experience.
studies that led to the Cooperative Curriculum Project, a
was given to an adequate description of scope. After long
up adopted a viewpoint which is reflected in the following

curriculum" is used to describe what is appropriate to be dealt with
distinctive from the term "content of curriculum" in that this latter
hat is in fact dealt with in the curriculum. "Scope" is the broader
may be dealt with; it includes more than can possibly be used in
ent" is the narrower term; it refers to what *is* to be dealt with.
escribe the field over which the church has legitimate purview for
and from which the church may appropriately draw the content

individual actions resulting from a program plan under church guidance directed toward attaining a church's mission. The actions have to do with performing the functions of the church: worship, proclamation and witness, nurture and education, and ministry to the whole world.

Now let us note how the two segments of the church program are related.

On the one hand, the learning experiences in the curriculum lead persons to
worship, witness, minister, and apply the gospel. In fact, we teach and train in
order that these actions may result. In the measure that a Christian education
curriculum plan does not move learners to engage in these activities, it is a
failure. On the other hand, the performance activities are often dependent on
the curriculum plan. That is, they call for teaching and training. For example, if
persons are to worship effectively, they need education in the nature, importance, and skills of worship. The case with any of the other performance activities would be similar.

Thus curriculum and performance activities are interrelated as cause and
effect. Curriculum leads to activity, and activity leads to curriculum.

Another angle of the relationship between program and curriculum has particular point in the case of the author's own denomination. Most Southern
Baptist churches have at least two program organizations, and a great many of
them have five: Sunday School, Church Training, Woman's Missionary Union,
Brotherhood, and the organized Music Ministry. Since the activities of these
five organizations need to be brought into proper correlation, the idea of a
correlated church program is highly important. Also, since each of these five
organizations has its own curriculum plans, these plans need to be brought
together into appropriate correlation; otherwise duplication, imbalance, poor
sequence, and even conflict could result.

The Question of Objectives

Here, of course, we are dealing with the question of what it is we are seeking
to accomplish through Christian education curriculum. Our task is so demand-
ing and the results are so important, that it behooves us to know exactly what
we are aiming for.

Well-defined objectives are essential to the best preparation and evaluation
of teaching materials. The educational leadership of the local church wants to
be able to trust its denominational publishing house to design curriculum
plans and produce related materials which will make possible, when properly
used, an effective program of teaching and training. Editors and program plan-

ners connected with the publishing house need to have before them, in all of their planning, producing, and testing of materials, the best possible statement of objectives. If local leaders are informed of the objectives which furnish guidance to editors, planners, and writers, they will use with much greater confidence and effectiveness the programs and materials which they obtain from their publishing house.

As we face the question of how objectives should be determined, we begin with a basic principle: God has revealed himself and his will to humanity. The record of that revelation is found in the Bible, and its culmination is found in the person of Jesus Christ. A study of the Bible leads us to the conviction that God himself has determined the greatest objective. He has had a purpose of redemptive grace from all eternity. Toward that objective he has been progressively working through all the long centuries. He has included us in his plan of the ages, and the greatest thrill of human existence is to share with him in the forwarding of that plan. Here, then, is the clue to the objectives of Christian education. By discovering what God is seeking to accomplish in and through the lives of persons and in and through his church, we will be prepared to face the question of how we can catch step with him and move in the direction he is moving.

There are two areas of concern for which we need Christian education objectives. One is the individual; the other is the church. God has purposes for both, and we must keep that fact in mind as we proceed.

From the time of Paul Vieth's pioneering volume, *Objectives in Religious Education*,[1] until the present, many efforts have been made to formulate an adequate and accurate statement of objectives. Practically all of the denominations, as well as other groups, have worked at the matter and issued a variety of statements.[2] Our purpose here, however, is not to review these statements but to deal with the nature, relationships, and uses of objectives.

Many leaders in the field of Christian education now believe it possible and desirable to state the curriculum objective in terms of a single, overarching goal. Such a statement points to the ultimate end or intention of a church's total curriculum. It encompasses the educational activities for every age level in every church program organization. The common acceptance and application of such an educational objective helps bring all phases of the total curriculum into proper relationship.

The objective which guided the Cooperative Curriculum Project was based on the conviction that it is not only possible but actually more desirable to have just one objective, extensive and comprehensive enough to include all that is attempted in Christian education. This objective was stated as follows:

The objective for Christian education is that a
self-disclosure, especially his redeeming love a
respond in faith and love—to the end that they
human situation means, grow as sons of God
the Spirit of God in every relationship, fulfill th
abide in the Christian hope.[3]

From the standpoint of the authors of
a very serious fault. It apparently assu
of God," whereas the true evangelica
in Christ Jesus by the power of the H
God. However, the statement has m
significant influence of helping to cd
value of a single objective.

We have said that there are two
tives: the individual and the chur
individuals alone. The New Testa
the church has a place of sublime

In the basic design paper for t
A) are found a statement of the
cational or curriculum objective

The mission of a church, com
mitment to Jesus Christ as Sav
the power of the Holy Spirit,
clamation and witness, nurt
God's purpose may be achie

This statement is broad
provided for in a church's
provided for in its progra
pose for the church's tot
ates in the community o
churches. Southern Ba
serve as "the basic ya
are measured. As this
lating factor to keep
purpose."

There is no desire
tion is that it shoul
leaders to understa

The edu
riculum ma

To he
Christ,
meaning
in consc
Christian

This object
intention is t
activities shou

The technica
dictionary defin
itself." The scop
the curriculum.
course, but it rea
The scope of
Bible for its basis
tional ministry tha
readers may wish
Although the Bib
curriculum, scope,
in the curriculum. T
but as broad as hum
In the curriculum
great deal of though
consideration the gr
statement:

The term "scope of
in the curriculum. It i
term has to do with
term; it refers to wha
the curriculum. "Con
Scope may be said to
its educational ministr
for its curriculum.[4]

The Cooperative Curriculum Project defined scope as "the whole field of relationships in the light of the gospel." It identified the elements of scope as these:

> The Christian experience of man under God—the divine dimension of reality in light of the gospel
> The Christian experience of man's relation to man—the human dimension of reality in light of the gospel
> The Christian experience of man within the world—the natural dimension of reality in light of the gospel.[5]

Here three elements of scope are identified. Actually, the preliminary study group identified four: God, man, nature, and history. These are the dimensions of human experience (the divine, the human, the natural, and the historical) and all of these are included in the scope of Christian education curriculum.

There is, however, another factor which must not be overlooked; in fact, it is the clue to the entire matter. Scope is the "whole field of relationships *in the light of the gospel.*" That is, in Christian education curriculum, while every phase of human experience may be explored, it is all done from the standpoint of God's self-disclosure and seeking love in Jesus Christ. Only in that way can a curriculum really be Christian. As Wyckoff has said, "the normative dimension of Christian education is the divine revelation."[6]

Wyckoff goes on to explain: "This is true because through revelation God has provided man with the necessary perspective from which to see the essential meaning and significance of the other dimensions. Our perception of our world in the light of the gospel means that we hear the word of God, witnessed to in the Bible and the church, spoken about in the dimensions of existence. Nature, man, and history remain in essence obscure, purposeless, and evil until they are seen and accepted in the light of God's self-disclosure in his Word and his redemptive action on man's behalf in the gospel of his seeking love in Jesus Christ. In this sense the scope of the curriculum is the word of God."[7]

In the Cooperative Curriculum Project, scope was dealt with in terms of *areas of curriculum.* These areas represent various facets or viewpoints of scope. Each area manifests the essential quality of the entire scope, and taken together the several areas comprise the scope. The areas make it possible for curriculum planners to deal with the scope in manageable portions.

When the educational objective was analyzed, five major facets emerged. These facets constitute the curriculum areas. Each one is distinctive, and each one is essential to the whole. They are (1) the human situation; (2) God's self-disclosure; (3) God's purpose of redemption; (4) the Christian's response in terms of faith, obedience, and discipleship; and (5) the Christian's effective experience in the church and its mission. Each of these facets reflects the three dimensions of reality with which every human being is concerned—the divine, the human, and the natural.

Further work was done to identify under each area the themes which comprehend "the major lifelong motifs in the Scope as seen from the perspective of that area."[8]

Here are the five areas of scope with their constituent themes.[9]

> LIFE AND ITS SETTING: THE MEANING AND EXPERIENCE OF EXISTENCE. The themes within this area are: Man Discovering and Accepting Himself; Man Living in Relationship with Others; Man's Relation to the Natural Order; Man's Involvement in Social Forces; Man's Coping with Change and the Absolute; Man's Creativity Within Life's Daily Routines.
>
> REVELATION: THE MEANING AND EXPERIENCE OF GOD'S SELF-DISCLOSURE. The themes within this area are: God Speaks in Man's Search for Meaning Beyond Himself; The Living God Seeks Man; The Gracious God Judges and Redeems; The Sovereign God Dwells with Man; God Speaks to Man Through the Scriptures; God Acts Through the Church to Make Himself Known; God Speaks to Man Through the Natural Order.
>
> SONSHIP: THE MEANING AND EXPERIENCE OF REDEMPTION. The themes within this area are: God's Redeeming Love for Man; Man's Responding to God's Redemptive Action; Becoming a New Person in Christ; Growing Up in Christ; Finding Identity in the Christian Community; The Christian's Hope Rests in the Triumphant God.
>
> VOCATION: THE MEANING AND EXPERIENCE OF DISCIPLESHIP. The themes within this area are: God's Call to Responsible Decision: Called to Serve One's Neighbor; The Stewardship of Life and Work; Discipline in the Christian Life; Joined in Discipleship in the World; Toward the Kingdom of God.
>
> THE CHURCH: THE MEANING AND EXPERIENCE OF CHRISTIAN COMMUNITY. The themes within this area are: Christians Are Bound Together in God's Love; God's Continuing Action in and Through His People; The Church Permeating Society; Extending Reconciliation and Redemption; The Church Lives by Worship; The Christian Community Mobilizing for Mission; Preparing and Equipping for Ministry.

One point about these five areas or broad themes was made very clear and emphatic in the report of the Cooperative Curriculum Project, namely, that the areas are not to be regarded as separate slices of the scope, but rather as vantage points for viewing the total scope.

Many denominations have made use of this approach to scope in designing their curriculum frameworks. Although Southern Baptists have used it somewhat, they take another approach to scope which is made necessary by the distinctive nature of their five program organizations: Sunday School, Church

Training, Music Ministry, Brotherhood, and Woman's Missionary Union. They use the term "curriculum area" to refer to an aspect of the total educational responsibility assigned to one of their church program organizations. (See Appendix A.) The Sunday School is responsible for teaching the Bible. Church Training is responsible for teaching and training in the areas of Christian theology and Baptist doctrine, Christian ethics, Christian history, church polity and organization, and equipping church members for discipleship and personal ministry. Brotherhood and Woman's Missionary Union are responsible for teaching missions. In addition, The Brotherhood is also responsible for developing personal ministry. The Music Ministry is responsible for developing musical skills, attitudes, and understandings.

Where Does the Curriculum Function?

For Christian education to take place there must be a learner, but the learner is never in isolation. The learner's "surroundings" are of great importance. There are environments conducive to Christian learning, and there are other environments which are hostile to it.

The proper surrounding or *context* for Christian education is the life and work of the church as it worships, witnesses, teaches, learns, ministers to human need, and applies the gospel to every area of life. The church is where the curriculum functions.

In a very real sense the church includes the Christian home. For many persons the family is the primary setting in which Christian learning takes place. Thus the Christian family may be thought of as the church in microcosm, and as such, it is of the greatest importance to the Christian experience and growth of its members. When the family circle is a fellowship of Christian love, it is easy for both children and adults to have Christian learning experiences.

The significance of the locale of Christian education curriculum can hardly be overemphasized. The communication of the faith requires an active, vital community of Christian believers that is reaching out as an instrument of God's redeeming love. This is the situation in which the eternal realities of the gospel will meet the life needs of learners. Here is where real Christian learning takes place. The more nearly a church can approximate what a true church of Jesus Christ should be, the more effective its witness and education become. If a church does not effectively demonstrate the reality and power of the faith it seeks to communicate, its efforts will be contradicted by its own failure to be a church.

Characteristics of Good Curriculum

A good curriculum for Christian education in the local church has at least seven characteristics:

1. *Biblical and theological soundness* are important to assure that what is taught in the curriculum is genuine Christianity.

2. *Relevance* has to do with suiting the teaching to the nature and needs of the learners in their current situation.

3. *Comprehensiveness* means that the curriculum will include all that is essential in the scope and all that is essential to the development of well-rounded Christian personality on the part of learners.

4. *Balance* means that the curriculum will have neither overemphasis nor underemphasis of the various parts that make it up.

5. *Sequence* is the presentation of portions of curriculum content in the best order for learning.

6. *Flexibility* is important if the curriculum is to be adaptable to the individual differences of the learners, adaptable to churches of different types, and adaptable to the varying abilities of leaders and teachers.

7. *Correlation* is the proper relation of part to part in the total curriculum plan.

How Shall the Curriculum Be Organized?

As this chapter has indicated, there are many factors to be considered in the design of a curriculum plan. These factors include the mission of the church, the educational objective, the scope, the learners, and methodology. As we view these important elements in curriculum design, we confront several important questions: How can the essential elements be brought together in proper synthesis? How can we assure that each of these elements is properly reflected in the total curriculum plan as well as in its several parts? How can we plan so that the curriculum will actually "come alive" in the experience of learners?

The answers to these questions are found in the concept of an *organizing principle.* This technical phrase may be explained as follows: An organizing principle is the rationale for the approach curriculum builders take to assure the proper relation of the design elements in a curriculum plan. The organizing principle is also a valuable instrument for testing the curriculum plan to see that it has in it the essential elements of design in proper relationship.

The organizing principle which guides Southern Baptist curriculum planners is *the involvement of learners in a meaningful exploration of the realities of the Christian faith and life in such a way that they move toward attaining the educational objective. This is done in the context of the church's life and work.*

It will be seen that this organizing principle reflects the following elements of curriculum design:

1. The educational objective ("in such a way that they move toward attaining the educational objective").

2. The scope ("the realities of the Christian faith and life").

3. Learners ("learners . . . in the context of the church's life and work").

4. Methodology ("the involvement of learners in a meaningful exploration . . ."). Inherent in the methodology theory are some matters which will receive detailed attention in the next chapter. These are (1) the lifelong learning task—"the involvement of learners," and (2) age-level activities—"meaningful exploration."

By way of summary, let us recall that we have set forth some basic elements of curriculum philosophy. We have dealt with the nature of curriculum itself in terms of learning experiences. We have considered how curriculum is related to program and to performance activities. We have examined the question of objectives both in regards to the church and in regards to the individual learner. We have looked at scope, or what the curriculum includes. We have defined the context, or the locale in which the curriculum functions. We have listed seven characteristics of a good curriculum. And finally, we have explained the organizing principle which brings all of these elements into proper relationship. It should now be quite evident that the indispensable factor in Christian education curriculum is *the involvement of learners in the educational process itself.*

By now the root system of your church's curriculum may have become quite meaningful. We hope that before you reach the end of chapter 4, it will become even more impressive.

Notes

1. (New York: Harper & Bros., 1930), pp. 80-88. Vieth had seven objectives. These related to God, Jesus Christ, Christlike character, constructive participation in the social order, a Christian philosophy of life, the church, and the use of "the best religious experience of the race" (p. 88).

2. For an account of the formulation of objectives in recent Protestant education, see D. Campbell Wyckoff, *The Gospel and Christian Education* (Philadelphia: The Westminster Press, 1959), pp. 120-25;

and Lawrence C. Little's chapter, "The Objectives of Protestant Religious Education," in *Religious Education: A Comprehensive Survey,* ed. Marvin Taylor (Nashville; Abingdon Press, 1960).

   3. *The Church's Educational Ministry,* p. 8.

   4. Ibid., p. 12.

   5. Ibid., p. 15.

   6. Wyckoff, *The Gospel and Christian Education,* p. 126.

   7. Ibid., p. 126 f.

   8. *The Church's Educational Ministry,* p. 18.

   9. Ibid., pp. 18-24.

4
Curriculum Design:
From Learning Tasks to Learning Outcomes

To Robert J. Havighurst of the University of Chicago we are indebted for a very significant advance in our understanding of human nature and the developing individual. In his *Human Development and Education*,[1] he presents the thesis that every human being has certain "developmental tasks" which he must undertake at the proper stage of his growth from childhood, through adolescence, to adulthood. At each stage of life the individual faces imperative tasks, the performance of which are prerequisite to his further development. If he succeeds with them, he grows and is thus prepared for the next level of experience. If he does not, his development toward maturity is retarded.

Educators quite generally accept Havighurst's thesis. One important inference to be drawn from it is that the chief responsibility of an educator is to help the individual undertake the tasks that are appropriate to him and to help him succeed with them. This accords with the basic principle that teaching consists in the guidance of learning.

The Lifelong Learning Task

Influenced by Havighurst's studies, Christian educators have developed the idea of "learning tasks" in Christian education. The idea of learning tasks, says Campbell Wyckoff, "has proved to be extremely useful and adaptable to Christian education." But he also points out that "the developmental aspect of the concept has required modification" in its application to Christian education.[2]

Some time after Dr. Havighurst had developed the idea of developmental tasks, he wrote a paper on the applicability of that concept to the concerns of Christian education. He held that there are no specific Christian developmental tasks, but that there are Christian ways of handling certain of the regular developmental tasks. This led to the discovery that there are certain processes through which learning takes place at every stage of a person's life. Three important words sum up these processes: (1) exploring, (2) discovering, and (3) appropriating. That is to say:

First, the person seeks to find out about himself and his surroundings. This is *exploration.*

Second, the person finds the meaning and value of himself and of the field of interest which he is exploring. This is *discovery.*

Third, the person makes the meaning and value of the new fact or idea a part of himself. This is *appropriation.* Furthermore, at every point in these processes, the learner has the task of "assuming personal and social responsibility."

The context or "operative environment" in which the learner explores, discovers, and appropriates meaning and value is "the field of relationships." That field is God, humanity, nature, and history; for every human being stands in a relationship to these four great entities, and Christian education has to do with the total person. Thus the scope of Christian education is the whole field of relationships in light of the gospel of Jesus Christ. Our goal is to bring persons into right and meaningful relations with God, with themselves and society, with the world of nature, and with the cultural heritage which has come to them from the past. Personality is always the result of interaction between the individual and the field of relationships; and in the development of Christian personality we deal with these relationships *in light of the gospel.* This is true throughout the learner's life span, because each of the Christian learning tasks is lifelong.

In summary: Christian learning is like general learning in that it involves the processes of exploring, discovering, and appropriating meaning and value. But it differs in that it adds to those processes the indispensable dimension of the Christian gospel. As a result, Christian learning is distinctive in four essential respects:

1. The field of relationships includes God and begins with God.
2. The thrust of the gospel affects every part of the process.
3. The Holy Spirit does his work in and through learning tasks that are distinctively Christian.
4. The learner assumes personal and social responsibility in light of the gospel.

These facts are relevant not only to the initial learning of the gospel but also to any and all relearning that may and ought to occur throughout the learner's life span.

Five learning tasks in Christian education are important enough to be pursued through an individual's entire life span. Because of the nature of these tasks, they are not called "developmental" but "lifelong." These tasks are as follows:

- Listening with growing alertness to the gospel and responding in faith and love
- Exploring the whole field of relationships in the light of the gospel
- Discovering meaning and value in the field of relationships in the light of the gospel
- Appropriating that meaning and value personally
- Assuming personal and social responsibility in the light of the gospel[3]

However, as we study the relation of these five tasks to one another, we discover that in reality there is but one task. The other four are continuing activities by which that one task is undertaken. The one task is the first in the list. *To listen with growing alertness to the gospel and respond in faith and love* is the one thing every human being needs to do throughout his life.

We see, then, that by lifelong learning task is meant a great, overall, purposeful activity engaged in by learners from early childhood through all the stages of the life span. The approach to Christian education in terms of a lifelong learning task is one of the most valuable elements of the newer developments in the field.

As a specific example of how the idea of a lifelong learning task applies, let us consider a statement produced by the authors' denomination in relation to the study of the Bible. From the human perspective, the one great lifelong learning task related to the biblical revelation is: *seeking with growing interest and devotion to understand God's revelation through his Word and responding to him in faith, love, and obedience.*[4] Encompassed in this task is the learning of Bible truth which leads to a conversion experience, and beyond that there is the spiritual growth appropriate to each stage of Christian development.

Note how this task involves the learner in the total scope of God's revelation through the Bible. In the Bible we see God in his relationships to human beings, to his created universe, and to history. We see the human person as he was created (in the image of God), as he now is in his broken relationship with God through pride and disobedience (a sinner), and as he can become in redemption (a child of God, a new creation). We see the supreme revelation of God through his Son, reconciling sinful persons to God and breaking down the barriers which separate persons from each other.

Every person's lifelong task is to recognize that God has given each person this supreme revelation and to seek to understand it and respond to it. Since no one can grasp the whole of God's revelation, this is a learning task for the entire life span as the learner is helped by the Holy Spirit increasingly to understand that revelation. Yet very young children can have experiences related to this task.

The result of this growing understanding should be a growing response to God in faith, love, and obedience. Obviously, such response is also lifelong. No one comes to the point where he has learned all there is to know of God's self-revelation. The learner continues to discover additional areas of his life in which he needs to trust, love, and obey God more completely.

There are a number of advantages in making the approach to Christian education through the concept of a lifelong learning task.

1. It makes the learner central in the learning process. The soundness of this approach is obvious.

2. It helps curriculum planners properly to relate the various elements of the curriculum plan. Subject matter, the needs of learners, church goals, and actions are brought together in the most appropriate way.

3. It assists writers of curriculum material appropriately to relate subject matter to learner needs.

4. It assists leaders and teachers in the local church properly to relate subject matter to learner needs.

5. It helps churches make their educational ministry more dynamic and relevant to life.

6. It helps learners to become involved in a meaningful exploration of curriculum areas.

In a word, by means of learning tasks, learners are involved in activities in which their persistent life needs are met by the abiding realities of the gospel. The learning task approach also eliminates the objection which is sometimes directed at "age-level objectives." The latter tend to put learning in terms of a meaningless average, not taking into account the important fact of individual differences on the part of learners. With the learning task approach, learners can progress at their own rates, according to their individual endowments, capacities, and readiness for learning.

Continuing Learning Activities

We have already pointed out that the lifelong learning task finds expression in continuing learning activities. These activities are also to be engaged in throughout life. To use technical language, they have "peaks of relevancy" across the life span. They are intermediate steps between lifelong learning tasks and specific age-level learning activities.

Again choosing our illustration with reference to the biblical revelation, we note that the lifelong learning task has four related continuing learning activities:

- Exploring the content of God's revelation as recorded in the Bible
- Discovering meaning, value, and relevance in the biblical revelation
- Appropriating personally the meaning and value of the biblical revelation
- Applying to all of one's relationships the meaning, value, and relevance of the biblical revelation

The first continuing activity, *exploring*, involves such things as reading, studying, comparing, searching, hearing, discussing, and meditating. Such activity is necessary to the understanding of the revelation. Spiritual truth is discerned with the mind, but above all with the spirit, as one is guided by the Holy Spirit.

The second activity grows naturally out of the first. It is *discovering*. The Bible is not a book of abstract truths. It is our guide to life here and hereafter. So the exploration of its content must lead to the discovery of meaning, value, and relevance. Meaning in this case is the underlying significance of what we find in the Bible. Having made this discovery with the help of the Holy Spirit, we ask, What is the value of this meaning? Having discovered meaning and value in the divine message, we are in position to consider its relevance to life today. As time and circumstances change, we will discover relevance that has not previously been apparent.

The third continuing learning activity, growing out of exploration and discovery, is *appropriating*. Meaning, value, and even relevance may stop short of personal acceptance; all too often they do. In such cases the student fails to receive in a personal way the redeeming truth which the Bible reveals. The person fails to respond to God in faith, love, and obedience. Yet the Holy Spirit is ever seeking to lead him to make the truth his own and to respond positively to God in Christ. This personal appropriation of saving truth, this life-transforming response to Christ, is more than a single event in the learner's life. When the Holy Spirit has his way, it is a continuing experience. It is rightly called a continuing learning activity.

The fourth activity, closely related to appropriation of truth, is *applying the truth to all of one's relationships*. Such application is a very personal matter; it must be made by the learner under the guidance of the Holy Spirit, though the aid of some human instrumentality is often needed. The task involves the learner in assuming personal and social responsibility for the truth learned. And it must deal primarily with personal relationships, that is, (1) one's relationship with God, (2) one's relationship with himself, and (3) one's relationship with others.

Besides these interpersonal relationships, there are two other relationships to which the learner must make personal application of truth: (1) a relationship to his physical environment and the natural world (the universe), and (2) a relationship to history, the life which has gone before. Only when we see God as the Lord of all the universe can we become good stewards of his good creation. Only when we see God as Lord of all history can we adequately discern his purposes and find our place within them.

As learners seek to put into practice the meaning, value, and relevance which they have discovered through exploring the content of the biblical revelation, they will be carrying out the response of faith, love, and obedience to God.

Because the point is highly important to a proper understanding of continuing learning activities, let us stress again that they are relevant throughout the life span. Learners are never to cease exploring the various curriculum areas within the scope of Christian education; they are constantly to be discovering meaning and value, appropriating personally that meaning and value, and assuming personal and social responsibility for the meaning and value of what they learn.

Four advantages in the use of the continuing-learning-activity approach in Christian education may be mentioned:

1. Continuing learning activities furnish a basis for selecting and using subject matter. They help us to come up with the right answers to the question, What is to be taught and why?

2. They suggest approaches to the effective involvement of learners in the lifelong learning task.

3. They aid in the development of teaching-learning units. Such units form the basis of the quarterlies and books by which the curriculum plan is conveyed to churches, their leaders, teachers, and learners.

4. They form the basis for developing appropriate age-level activities. To a consideration of such activities let us now turn.

Age-Level Learning Activities

An age-level activity is an expression of a continuing learning activity which is appropriate for a given age level. We are able to determine suitable age-level activities by applying age-level readiness (see pp. 61-62) to continuing learning activities.

In some respects age-level activities can hardly be distinguished from age-level learning methods. In general, however, an age-level activity is broader than a learning method and may be expressed through several specific learning methods. For example, an age-level activity might be described by such words as participating, investigating, discovering, and encountering. But learners might participate in any one of those broad actions through such methods as reading, participating in group discussion, listening to a lecture, or interviewing an authority on the subject.

In order to clarify further the nature and value of age-level learning activities, we present some abbreviated examples from one of the age divisions, Youth. Note below that all of these Youth learning activities are related to the lifelong learning task of seeking with growing interest and devotion to understand God's revelation through his Word and responding to him in faith, love, and obedience. They are arranged so as to show also their relation to the continuing learning activities.

Youth Learning Activities

  I. Exploring the content of God's revelation as recorded in the Bible
       1. Determining the meaning of Bible passages for those for whom they were originally intended
       2. Discovering God's meaning of biblical truth for today
 II. Discovering increasing meaning, value, and relevance in the biblical revelation
       1. Relating Bible statements to science and to other bodies of knowledge
       2. Assigning appropriate weight to the various sections of the Bible
III. Appropriating personally the meaning and value of the biblical revelation
       1. Evaluating life experiences for help in attaching meaning to Bible content
       2. Drawing upon Bible content in developing a philosophy of life
 IV. Applying to all of one's relationships the meaning, value, and relevance of the biblical revelation
       1. Practicing prayer as a real factor in applying God's truth to life
       2. Considering seriously all one's relationships and decisions in light of Bible teachings

Similar examples could be given for each of the other age divisions.

What now, we may ask, are the advantages of such statements of age-level activities? We mention three:

1. They enable curriculum planners to select appropriate content for persons of a given age level.

2. They enable teachers and leaders to choose methods and procedures by which learners may explore meanings and experiences in any given curriculum area. The examples cited are related to learning the biblical revelation, but others could be listed which are suitable for learning Christian doctrine, ethics, history, missions, hymnody, and the various skills involved in Christian training.

3. They enable us to identify changes or learnings that take place in the life of a learner as a result of his engaging in those activities.

Age-Level Scope

Age-level scope is that portion of the total scope which is appropriate to be dealt with at a learner's given age level. As was pointed out in chapter 3, in curriculum terminology, scope refers to what is appropriate to be dealt with, whereas content refers to what is actually dealt with. But before curriculum planners can know what content to use in teaching-learning units for a given age group, they must know the scope from which suitable choice may be made. Therefore, they determine in advance what are the limits of the scope for early childhood, elementary years, youth, and adults.

L. Harold DeWolf, a theologian and also an experienced Sunday School teacher, expressed the conviction that

> we ought to teach the whole range of the scope at all age levels, though assuredly the manner, detail, and depth of the instruction will vary greatly . . . . The longer I have taught at both senior and adult levels, the more firmly convinced I am that the *whole* gospel must be taught at each of these levels, almost as if it had never been taught before. So new is the emotional, volitional, and ideational context at each of these levels that the gospel itself is likely to appear now as a great mystery and even novelty.[5]

But while we may agree with this general principle, yet, as DeWolf himself suggests, the manner in which the scope of the curriculum is treated greatly depends on the age group with which we are dealing.

In *The Church's Educational Ministry: a Curriculum Plan,* which is one of the richest and fullest compendiums of Christian education resources yet compiled, each of the themes in the total scope is dealt with in terms of its significance for the respective age levels. In each instance the first item treated is "Meanings and experiences within this theme relevant for this age level," and the explanation is given that "This is content, a selected part of Scope."

Here are a few excerpts from the scope statements for just one of the areas, "God's Redeeming Love for Man." Note in these statements that the content includes both meanings and experiences. This is right because scope is more than subject matter; it always includes experience in relation to subject matter.

Statement of Theme

Through God's changeless and seeking love for man, supremely manifested in Jesus Christ (his life, death, resurrection, and ascension) redemption is made possible whereby man's alienation from God is overcome and the way is opened for him to be reconciled with God. Thus man's persistent need for reconciliation, meaning, acceptance, integrity, security, and freedom is adequately met.

EARLY CHILDHOOD
   God loves us and wants us to love and obey him.
   Jesus shows us what God's love is like.

ELEMENTARY YEARS
   God, who created us, loves us and intends that we should love and obey him.
   God has shown us his love for us in the life, death, resurrection, and ascension of Jesus Christ.

YOUTH
   God's redeeming love for man manifest from creation on is supremely manifested in Jesus Christ (his incarnation, life, crucifixion, resurrection, ascension). In the incarnation, God identified himself with man and offered himself that man might be redeemed.
   God holds man responsible for his choice to accept or reject his redeeming love.

ADULTHOOD
   God's love and forgiveness do not obliterate the inevitable results of sin and evil, but enable man to redirect life in spite of these results.
   In his seeking love, God enables man to recognize his need for redemption and to express it through repentance and confession.

Age-Level Learning Readiness

Closely related to age-level scope are age-level readinesses. By age-level readinesses we mean the inherent capabilities of learners, including both their abilities and tendencies. By *general readiness* we mean the expected capabilities (abilities and tendencies) of persons at each age level which are outgrowths of maturation and typical social experience. By *specific readinesses* we mean the capabilities of persons at each age level to become meaningfully involved in a particular curriculum area.

To illustrate this matter of age-level learning readiness, here are some examples from the theme used to illustrate age-level scope, namely, "God's Redeeming Love for Man." Before reading the next few paragraphs, reread the statement of the theme on page 61. Then, as you read what follows here, note that the statements identify the readiness of the learner for this theme in terms of basic needs, interests, motivations, capacities, and developmental tasks.

EARLY CHILDHOOD

The young child needs to be wanted, approved, and accepted.

The young child is able to perceive something of the love of God through parents and parent-figures who themselves are committed to God.

ELEMENTARY YEARS

The elementary child has a growing capacity to understand that God loves us and intends that we should love and obey him.

The elementary child has a capacity for beginning comprehension of the love of God as shown in the life, death, and resurrection of Jesus Christ.

YOUTH

Youth frequently have a sense of inadequacy, failure, and insecurity.

The young person is looking for the meaning and purpose of life.

Youth are at the stage of life where they have the intellectual capacity to recognize that God through his redemptive love manifested in the life, death, and resurrection of Jesus Christ has made forgiveness available to every person.

ADULTHOOD

A major drive in the adult years is for security which will reach into the future.

The responsibility for others that comes with adulthood makes adults open to appreciation of what God has done and is doing for them.[6]

Age-level readiness is used by curriculum designers and church leaders in the following ways:

1. To establish the optimum age at which to introduce various concepts.

2. To help determine the methods and activities to be used at each age level.

3. To help determine the proper sequence for presenting content through the life span.

4. To keep all educational organizations in the church consistent as to the concepts and approaches used with each age level.

Age-Level Methodology

The selection and use of appropriate methods in communicating the Christian message are matters of major concern to Christian teachers and leaders. If desirable changes in the lives of learners are to be brought about, the methods employed must be related to the ways persons learn; otherwise the methods may be worse than useless. An educational method is a means of achieving an educational end. It is a procedure used in a teaching-learning situation for the purpose of assisting persons to learn and change.

Age-level methodology has to do with that type of activity or procedure which is most effective in creating an appropriate learning situation for learners of a given age level. Age-level methods are practical ways of doing an age-level activity. Several age-level methods may be employed to do an age-level activity.

Listed on page 64 are some examples of age-level methods chosen from among many which could be named. The X's indicate the age levels for which the respective methods are suitable. X-minus means that the method is not suitable for the youngest members of the group.

Variety is a key word in relation to the selection of teaching-learning methods for both individual and group experiences. Each unit or session plan should suggest enough different methods that teachers may select those which seem appropriate for their group. Factors which determine "appropriate methods" include: (1) capabilities of the teacher or leader, (2) capabilities of the group, (3) size of the group, (4) meeting place, (5) availability of resources, (6) learning goals.

Learner Outcomes

In all of our teaching, we are "teaching for results."[7] That is, we are seeking outcomes in the learners' lives that represent desirable changes—changes that mean that the learners are fulfilling the learning tasks and moving toward the ultimate objective of Christian education.

The Church's Educational Ministry identifies desired learner outcomes for each of the themes. Taking the same theme we have already used in relation to age-level scope and age-level learning readiness, we note some possible outcomes of teaching "God's Redeeming Love for Man." For each age level, the following questions are raised: "What may the learner achieve within this

Age Levels

Methods	Preschool	Elementary	Youth	Adult
RESEARCH				
Case study		X	X	X
Listening	X	X	X	X
Picture study	X-	X	X	X
Scripture searching		X-	X	X
GROUP DISCUSSION				
Brainstorming		X-	X	X
Buzz groups (small groups)		X-	X	X
Conversation	X-	X	X	X
Interview-report		X	X	X
Panel-forum		X-	X	X
Pro-con discussion		X-	X	X
DRAMATIC TECHNIQUES				
Creative dramatics		X	X	X
Monologues		X-	X	X
Plays and skits		X-	X	X
ART ACTIVITIES				
Crafts		X	X	
Drawing	X-	X	X	X
Map-making		X-	X	X
MUSIC				
Analyzing		X	X	
Creating		X		
Listening	X	X	X	X
Singing	X-	X	X	X
CREATIVE WRITING				
Letters		X	X	X
Poems		X	X	X
Stories		X	X	X
FORMAL METHODS				
Book review		X-	X	X
Debate			X-	X
Forum		X	X	X
Lecture		X-	X	X
Memorization	X-	X	X	X
Research and report		X-	X	X
Storytelling	X-	X	X	X
Testing		X	X	X

theme in the fulfillment of the learning tasks? What are possible changes or learnings on the part of the learner that may result from his appropriation of the significance and value discovered? These changes or learnings may be associated with skills, attitudes, motivations, perceptions including understandings and appreciations.''

EARLY CHILDHOOD
The young child may achieve a beginning awareness that God loves everyone.
The young child may achieve a beginning awareness that Jesus shows us what God is like.

ELEMENTARY YEARS
The elementary child may achieve an awareness of the significance of Jesus' life, death, resurrection, and ascension.
The elementary child may achieve a desire for a personal relation with God who expressed his love for him in Christ.

YOUTH
Youth may achieve an understanding of forgiving love, making possible the forgiveness of sin.
Youth may achieve a confidence that God's redemptive love can make life whole and an acceptance of the fact that God's love brings true meaning and purpose to life.

ADULTHOOD
The adult may achieve realization of the meaning of redemption and a deepened loyalty to God in gratitude for his redemption in Christ.
The adult may achieve a realization that God's love enables persons to maintain a proper balance between the facts and struggles of daily life and the demands of Christian commitment.

In this chapter we have traced the pathway of learning from its beginning in the learning task to its desired result in learning outcomes. We have seen that involved in the process are continuing learning activities which persons of every age level need to pursue. We have also seen that there are distinctive age-level learning activities which are specifically related to age-level scope and specifically based on age-level learning readinesses. Finally we have noted some of the various age-level teaching-learning methods which may be employed by those who guide the learning process.

We cannot be sure that all persons who begin the learning process will manifest the desired outcomes in their lives. But God's Word does not return to him fruitless, and we can be sure that in many instances learners will enter upon the fullness of life in Christ Jesus and move more and more into the richness of experience and fruitfulness of service that God intends.

Intergenerational Activities

Now that we have examined the various aspects of learning in terms of age-level considerations, let us take a brief look at a different but very valid approach—intergenerational activities. A church's educational ministry should include such activities because of the need for the total community of faith to be taught as an ungraded group. All persons above the age of early childhood can and should participate collectively in such learning activities.

A competent teaching pastor—which every pastor ought to be—can, through the pulpit ministry, accomplish much to bring this about. Among other things, pulpit messages of educational quality can be designed for children and youth as well as for adults. In the sanctuary, models can actually be set for a Christian education ministry to all of the age groups at the same time so that everyone is included. Pastors may use their influence in other ways to promote intergenerational teaching and learning.

A church can provide for intergenerational learning in smaller groups. For example, some churches use "family clusters." A cluster consists of a group of perhaps a dozen persons, led by a member capable of guiding all of the age levels together. The twelve persons would include, say, four adults, four youths, and four children. Of course, the themes dealt with need to be within the range of each of the involved individual's interests and capacities.

Family cluster groups on some occasions may deal with matters of special interest to children; on other occasions, with matters of special interest to youth; and on yet other occasions, with matters of special interest to adults. In such a learning situation, every member of the group teaches, and each of the members can learn from what the others have to contribute. Often this is something very valuable. Thus an adult can learn from a child or a youth, and vice versa. In the case of some learners, certain educational outcomes may result which could not have been achieved in any other way.

To say the least, there is real educational value in persons of one age level coming to know and appreciate the thoughts and feelings of persons of other age levels. The results can strengthen not only the educational effectiveness of the church, but also its total life and work.

Notes

1. (New York: Longmans, Green & Co., 1953).
2. Wyckoff, *The Gospel and Christian Education*, p. 67.

3. *The Church's Educational Ministry*, p. 33.
4. For other examples of lifelong learning tasks, see Appendix A, p. 146.
5. Quoted in Wyckoff, p. 176.
6. For other examples of age-level readiness, see Appendix A, pp. 146-148.
7. This is the title of a helpful book by Findley B. Edge (Nashville: Broadman Press, 1956).

5
When Curriculum Comes to Life

A driver does not need to be a master mechanic to operate an automobile. With a little knowledge and skill, he can drive successfully for hundreds of trouble-free miles. However, the more he knows about the mechanical functioning of his automobile the more likely he is to obtain its maximum performance and to be able to service it when trouble develops.

Likewise, a church leader who understands the design of the curriculum will be able to use the materials more intelligently and to deal more creatively with opportunities and problems in specific learning situations. For example, although learning task concepts may be built into printed curriculum materials, Sunday School teachers will be able to select teaching goals and methods much more intelligently if they have a clear understanding of the lifelong learning tasks, continuing learning activities, and age-level activities.

However, one does not have to understand completely *all* of the elements in the curriculum design to benefit from those elements in guiding class members in growth-generating learning experiences. The principal function of some of the design elements is to guide denominational leaders who develop curriculum materials and other religious educators who interpret curriculum. Thus, as ingredients of a cake are not individually identifiable in the final product, some elements in the curriculum design are built into the printed curriculum materials although they may not be obviously discernable in the printed quarterly.

But volunteer church leaders in Christian education do need a thorough understanding of at least two crucial components in a curriculum plan. They are the curriculum framework and curriculum resource materials. Volunteer Christian educators also need to understand and be able to guide curriculum in action.

The Curriculum Framework—A Long-Range Plan of Study

A curriculum design is expressed in one or more curriculum frameworks. A curriculum framework, in turn, is expressed in specific quarterlies and other kinds of curriculum materials. A framework is a long-range plan for organizing proposed learning experiences related to the content of the curriculum.

Two concepts in this definition need special clarification. They are content and long-range plan.

The content is basic realities explored and experienced by learners participating in the curriculum itself. The essence of Christian education content is truths about God and his relationship to man. The content of the curriculum includes such great realities as God, Christ, sin, salvation, sanctification, and eternity. Thus, a lesson entitled "God's Love Revealed in Christ" is not essentially a study of a Bible passage and a lesson writer's exposition and application of that passage. The content of the lesson is God's love *per se* as it is revealed in Christ.

However, the content of the curriculum is not limited to these basic realities. It may also include principles, problems, and conditions related to the Christian faith and life. For example, in studies dealing with prayer, or various aspects of Christian citizenship, or a Christian view of sex, the content is the particular principle, problem, or condition being studied.

Often people consider the printed lesson material to be the content. The printed lesson discussion is simply subject matter written by finite writers in an effort to describe one or more realities in the content. The content is the realities themselves; the exposition and application of these realities in a quarterly is subject matter.

This concept of content is essential if one is to understand religious curriculum materials and to use them creatively. Lesson quarterlies and teacher's guides are never ends within themselves. The most they can claim to be is catalytic agents designed, with the help of the Holy Spirit, to help learners and leaders explore for themselves the great Christian realities to which the materials are pointing. If teachers and other church leaders accept this concept of content, they are never circumscribed by what they consider to be the limitations of the printed materials.

A second concept in the definition of curriculum framework needing clarification is long-range plan. There must be some system of organizing any kind of educational experiences. One plan for organizing proposed curriculum experiences might be to study in alphabetical sequence the great realities of the Christian faith. Although this plan has obvious weaknesses, one has to admit that it is a plan.

Denominational editors, in developing curriculum frameworks, seek to use relevant insights from education and psychology as well as the Christian faith itself. They seek to develop a definite plan for the study of Christian realities which is meaningful to the age group for whom they are preparing materials. Special consideration is given to the needs and interests of learners. Thus they seek to relate in a definite plan of study the realities of the Christian faith and the needs and concerns of individuals who will participate in the curriculum.

A curriculum framework is expressed in the form of a series of unit themes so developed as to guide learners over a period of one or more years to explore significant aspects of the Christian faith. The entire framework has comprehensiveness. Over a predetermined period of time learners are guided in an exploration of a major segment of the Christian faith. A curriculum framework has balance. Areas to be studied are given adequate attention without slighting some and devoting too much time to others. A curriculum framework reflects sequence. Although learners are guided through successive units, there is continuity and progression in the total study plan.

Probably the most familiar curriculum plan in churches of all denominations is the Uniform Lesson system. Although, like any other plan, it has its weaknesses, the Uniform Lesson system is an excellent plan to use in illustrating a curriculum framework.

First, in the thinking of members of the Uniform Lesson committee, the Uniform Lesson system is more than a plan for studying biblical passages. It is a plan for exploring the great realities and truths recorded in the Bible. A study of the 1980-86 framework appearing on an accompanying page reveals that it is a six-year plan of study. Note that a study of the nature of the Bible is included in the framework. Also, almost every year a full quarter is given to a study of one of the Gospels. Each year there also is a balanced offering of Old Testament studies, New Testament studies, and studies of the great themes of the Christian faith. It is obvious even from a brief study of the framework that no unit is an end within itself. Each is a part of a well-organized, long-range plan of study.

Likewise, other types of denominational curriculum materials are expressions of long-range, well-organized curriculum frameworks. To understand an individual unit or lesson, one needs to understand the curriculum framework, or long-range plan, of which it is a part.

UNIFORM LESSON CYCLE
1980-86
Arrangement of Quarters According to the
Calendar Year December Through November

1980-1981	1981-1982	1982-1983	1983-1984	1984-1985	1985-1986
December-February					
The Gospel of Matthew (21)*	The Person and Work of Jesus (20)	The Gospel of Luke (13)	Studies in Isaiah (13)	What The Bible Is (3)	Advent: To You A Savior (4)
				The Gospel of John (17)	Jesus Teaches About Living (9)
March-May					
Easter April 19	Easter April 11	The Book of Acts (13)	The Gospel of Mark (8)	Easter April 7	The Christian Hope (7)
The Book of Hebrews (5)	The Book of Revelation (6)	Easter April 3	Easter April 22	Studies in Wisdom Literature (6)	Easter March 30
			The Letter of James (5)		The Holy Spirit and the Church (5)
June-August					
The Book of Deuteronomy (13)	New Testament Personalities (13)	Old Testament Personalities (13)	The Rise and Fall of a Nation (13)	The Minor Prophets (13)	Jeremiah, Ezekiel, and Daniel (14)
September-November					
Great Passages of the Bible (13)	Origins of God's Chosen People (13)	Our Biblical Faith (13)	The Letters of Paul— Part I (13)	The Letters of Paul— Part II (13)	

*Parenthetical numerals indicate number of sessions

Curriculum Resource Materials—Guides and Resources in Study

When packages of curriculum materials are opened in a church, few members of that church realize how many thousands of hours have gone into the preparation of the attractively bound periodicals. A better understanding by church leaders of the background, contents, and intended uses of the materials can increase tremendously the usefulness of the materials in the life of the church.

Leaders need to understand, first of all, the nature and purpose of curriculum materials. As John the Baptist "was not the light, but came to bear witness to the light" (John 1:8, RSV), so curriculum materials are not intended to be accepted as final truth. Instead, they are guides and resources for use in a study of truth.

Leaders need also to understand the many kinds of curriculum materials available for use in their church and the specific helps offered in each quarterly. The curriculum in many churches is limited by the failure of that church to make available to the right persons picture sets, lesson commentaries, audiovisual aids, and other special materials prepared by the denomination to be used in the church curriculum.

Most church leaders know that certain materials are available for members and other materials are available for teachers. Many of them fail to realize, however, the vast resources available within the bounds of the specific periodicals. A teacher's guide, for example, may contain sections offering suggested teaching plans, background lesson material, articles on techniques of teaching and other aspects of group work, booklists and other recommended resources to be ordered or secured from a library, and many other valuable aids. Often valuable resources go unused as a reader limits through habit his use of a quarterly to one or two familiar sections.

Church leaders, especially teachers, need to keep in mind that the quarterlies are educational instruments in a long-range plan of study. On receiving a new quarterly, one of the first things they should do, therefore, is to see how the study materials for the quarter fit into the total plan of study. The location of the units in the framework, or the relationship of the unit in the quarterly to studies the preceding or following quarter, may be an important clue to the most intelligent use of the materials.

Finally, teachers need to preview carefully all the study materials for the quarter before they begin their preparation for an individual session. Gaining an overview of study plans for a unit or quarter can aid a teacher significantly in selecting aims and in relating each session to the broader plan of study.

Denominationally prepared curriculum materials are not intended to be restrictive. Creative teachers who have the time and resources are encouraged to supplement their regular curriculum materials with materials from other relevant sources. The teacher's goal is to guide learners in meaningful learning experiences. Curriculum materials are simply suggested instruments for the teacher to use intelligently in achieving that objective.

Curriculum—Relevant Learning Experiences

Thus far we have investigated the meaning of curriculum foundations, curriculum design, a curriculum framework, and curriculum materials. We have seen that the first three of these elements are expressed in the fourth—curriculum materials. Most of the work on all four of the elements are done by denominational personnel.

But are these curriculum itself? The answer is emphatically no. Curriculum, as interpreted by most educators today, is something which happens in an actual learning situation. It may be influenced by printed materials, but it is never to be equated with those materials. Curriculum is something which happens in life to normal human beings.

Let us consider a concrete example of curriculum in action. From this example, we will see what curriculum is and how it is related to curriculum materials.

A youth group in one church was studying a unit on race relations. The theme for one session was "Overcoming Racial Barriers in Our Community." Bill and Joe insisted that it would be a waste of time to discuss the topic as, they claimed, no racial barriers existed in their community. In an effort to prove their point, they cited integrated schools and open housing.

Although Mary, the discussion leader, had planned to have a panel discussion on the topic, she changed her plans when she saw Bill's reaction. She asked Joe, Bill, and three other members of the group to interview three black students each during the week. They were to ask their interviewees what, if any, racial barriers they experienced in the community, and they were to report on their interviews to the entire group the next Sunday night.

The reports the next Sunday night were a complete surprise to all of the members of the group. All black students interviewed cited numerous barriers, many subtle, to which the white youth were completely oblivious. One of the most frequent complaints was that white students in the local high school seemed to accept black students as fellow classmates but seldom did they show interest in them as persons. Consequently, the black students felt that they were tolerated as a group but not respected as human beings.

Most of the members of the church youth group were students in that high school. In the discussion which followed the interview reports, they resolved to work individually and as a group to tear down the wall which separated human beings in their own school.

In chapter 3, curriculum was said to be the sum of learning experiences. In the experiences of this church group, we find several kinds of learnings. All were integral parts of the curriculum. First, there was an acquisition of knowledge. They learned the fact of a racial barrier in their own school. This knowledge changed their attitude regarding their need for further work in this area. Their new knowledge and attitude gave them a deeper appreciation for problems faced by their fellow black students. Later, as they sought to overcome the racial barrier in their school, they developed certain skills in human relations. All of these learning experiences—knowledge, attitude, appreciation, and skills—were important parts of the curriculum.

But not all experiences a church group has are parts of the curriculum. To be a part of the curriculum, the experiences must be related generally to the curriculum plan. In the case of the church youth group, their learning experiences were related directly to a theme, or reality, proposed for study by their curriculum quarterly. This is not to say that the learning experiences must be directly related to the area for study on a given Sunday. The learning experiences may be related in a more general way to the content—the realities—included in the general curriculum plan.

To be a part of the curriculum, the experiences must be under church guidance. This does not mean that they must take place in the church building on Sunday. Although many valuable learnings come in this way, some of the most important learning takes place as learners, inspired during a class session, seek during the week to put into practice what they learned on Sunday. Thus learning inspired by the church may take place, or be reinforced, in the home, in business, at school, on the golf course, or in many other places. All of these are important parts of the church's curriculum.

Finally, to be a part of the curriculum, the learning experiences must be related generally to the church's objective of Christian education. Many churches do not have a formal statement of their Christian education objective. However, almost all churches have at least an overall intent in this area. Although their curriculum could be strengthened by the statement of an overall objective, learning experiences related to the general intent of the church in Christian education are parts of the church's curriculum.

In summary, curriculum in Christian education is the sum of all learning experiences resulting from a curriculum plan used under church guidance and directed toward attaining a church's objectives.

Practical Curriculum Problems

Academic definitions and illustrations sometimes do not communicate the full meaning of a concept. Additional understanding comes through a consideration of practical problems related to the implementation of the concept.

Church leaders frequently raise with denominational curriculum specialists problems related to curriculum. Answers to some of the more frequent and pertinent of these questions can further clarify the meaning of curriculum.

1. *"The curriculum materials do not deal with subjects of greatest interest to my class members at the times they are most interested in studying them."*

The personal interests of learners are highly important to teachers for two reasons. First, learning is easier and more lasting when it is related to the personal interests of learners. In addition, the interests of a learner are important clues to the kind of person he is and what his real needs are.

However, there is no necessary correlation between a person's immediate interests and deepest spiritual needs which should be met in a program of Christian education. Even when a learner expresses a sincere interest in one area of Christian education and a lack of interest in another area, it does not follow logically that that person should spend all available time studying in the area of major interest. For example, a person who has a genuine interest in personal evangelism should not spend all available time studying in this area. If this person develops as a well-balanced Christian, considerable time should be spent exploring ways the Christian faith can express itself in other areas of life.

Actually, one of the purposes of education is to create on the part of learners an awareness of needs and to cultivate new interests. No reputable school would build its curriculum entirely around the immediate interests of learners.

Basically, the clue to the curriculum should be the overarching objective of Christian education. This overarching objective finds expression in the curriculum framework and in specific curriculum materials. Therefore, if the church would maintain a balanced, purposeful, and constructive ministry of

Christian education, it needs to use its curriculum materials as general guides in planning and conducting learning experiences.

This is not to say that teachers should not give serious consideration to the interests of their class members. Earlier it was stated that these interests are valuable approaches to learning and clues to needs. Both factors need to be seriously considered by teachers.

Many times a study theme will be directly related to interests of learners. Even when such a relationship is not obvious, good teachers, in the way they approach the lesson or in the application they make, frequently can relate the study area to personal interests of learners.

Sometimes when learners express a special interest in studying in a certain area, the teacher, if he studies the curriculum framework, will find that the area in question is to be studied during a forthcoming quarter. In most cases, class members are willing to delay a study if they know that it is coming soon in the normal course of their curriculum plan.

On rare occasions, there is justification in deviating from the curriculum plan long enough to make a careful study of an area of special interest and need even though not in the curriculum framework, provided that interest or need is directly related to the overall objective of the church's program of Christian education.

2. *"I can't get my class members interested in serious study and discussion."*

A teacher facing this problem needs to spend considerable time in prayerful contemplation on the cause of the problem. The reason for the reluctance to engage in serious study and discussion may be the clue to solving the problem.

If the disinterest is symptomatic of spiritual frigidity and an excessive concern for the things of this world, the problem may not be solved until the class members have a greater awareness of the presence of God in their lives. There can be no meaningful study of stewardship until persons making the study have an awareness that "every good endowment and every perfect gift is from above, coming down from the Father of lights" (Jas. 1:17, RSV). Thus, claiming power and guidance from the Holy Spirit, the teacher needs to seek prayerfully, intelligently, and lovingly to help class members become more aware of the reality of God's love and concern for each of them.

Sometimes persons with deep spiritual perception engage in activities or develop attitudes inconsistent with the faith they profess. When they do this, serious study and discussion of the Christian faith may become a threat to

makes it possible for members of the class to help each other.

One of the best ways teachers can help class members is to demonstrate in their own lives the qualities they would like to help develop in the lives of class members. Teachers who demonstrate in personal experience the reality of spiritual resources during times of crisis, for example, teach far more than they do when they simply discuss those spiritual realities during a thirty-minute class session.

Finally, teachers who would meet the needs of class members must recognize the role of the Holy Spirit in the teaching process. In the final analysis, teachers alone cannot meet human needs. Only as they recognize the presence and power of the Holy Spirit and are used by the Spirit can they hope to make lasting contributions in the lives of their class members.

This brings into clear perspective the power which produces change through Christian curriculum. All that is done in developing curriculum designs, frameworks, materials, and lesson plans is of no avail until this work is used by the Holy Spirit.

He is the power which produces change in Christian education.

6
How People Learn

No study of curriculum is complete without a serious investigation of the learning process. Regardless of how good are the curriculum design, the curriculum materials, and even the teachers themselves, all of these fail unless learning takes place.

What Is Learning?

Since learning is the essential element in the educative process, it seems that there would be a clearly stated and generally accepted definition of what learning is. Unfortunately, this is not true. Educational psychologists themselves are not in agreement on what learning is or how it takes place. As one of them explained, educational psychologists, in the absence of positive knowledge of what learning is, develop theories of what they think it is.

On one point they are in agreement, however. Learning involves more than the acquisition of knowledge. By popular misconception, learning is the mathematical process of adding facts to one's store of knowledge. Although the acquisition of knowledge is one form of learning, learning itself is more like a chemical change than a mathematical process. In real learning, different elements are brought together, a reaction takes place, and the result is different from what either of the elements was before.[1]

In Christian education, this merging of elements to produce a new element is expressed in the theory of crossing points. According to this theory, learning occurs when an eternal truth of God crosses a persistent life need of a person. An example is the reality of God's love touching, or coming to bear upon, an individual's feeling of loneliness and special need. As a result, the individual learns that God is love.

Many kinds of learning result from crossing-point experiences. Christian attitudes, for example, cannot be developed through logical reasoning and sheer willpower alone. Certainly there are rational and emotional factors involved in the development of attitudes. Yet, in addition to these, spiritual resources outside oneself must enter the mind and heart before an attitude worthy to be called Christian can develop. A Christian attitude develops, therefore, when a spiritual reality crosses a persistent life need of an individual.

Likewise, traits of Christian character cannot be learned through human reasoning and effort alone. Awareness of personal need must somehow intersect spiritual truths and realities before Christian character traits are developed.

The crossing-point theory of learning assumes the existence of two areas of reality. First, there are God's eternal truths. These are spiritual realities such as God, salvation by grace through faith, and the efficacy of prayer. In addition, there are spiritual principles, instituted by God himself, such as the power of Christian love. Although these spiritual realities and principles cannot be seen with the naked eye, they are as real as life itself.

The crossing-point theory also recognizes the realities of human existence. Each person searches, struggles, hopes, wins victories, suffers, aspires, experiences frustration, fails and tries again. When an eternal truth of God crosses one of these human predicaments, learning takes place.

The purpose of Christian education, then, is to encourage crossing-point experiences. God's eternal truths cannot really be communicated simply as academic knowledge. Neither can one's human dilemma be explored successfully on a humanistic level. God's eternal truths and answers to a person's human problems are found only in relationship to each other.

This does not mean that every learning in Christian education is a discernible crossing of an eternal truth of God and a persistent need of a person. Learning the history of one's denomination, for example, can be a meaningful learning experience in Christian education, but it may not reflect in the immediate experience of the learner the crossing of an eternal truth of God and a persistent life need. However, the basic, life-changing Christian learnings do come in this way.

How Does Learning Take Place?

If learning occurs when an eternal truth of God crosses a persistent need of an individual, under what conditions do such crossings occur? This question brings us back to the learning tasks defined and discussed in chapter 4. Life-long learning tasks represent fundamental approaches by which finite persons interact with infinite realities in the Christian faith. (Review the discussion of learning tasks in chapter 4, and reflect on the interrelatedness of learning tasks and crossing points.) There is the need, however, to translate concepts of fundamental life experiences related to learning tasks and crossing points to recognizable human situations.

Let us consider, therefore, six familiar ways in which crossing points, with the help of the Holy Spirit, can be stimulated and significant learning might result.

1. *Christian Nurture*

Some of the most profound learning experiences in life take place, usually unconsciously and in an informal way, as one is associated with others in the human family and in the family of God, the church. It is generally agreed that these kinds of learning are the most basic and formative of all learning experiences in life.

Perhaps the greatest single need of a child (or an adult, for that matter) is to love and be loved. Formal discussions on how love expresses itself in specific situations can be helpful, but one cannot really learn to love simply by talking about it. One learns to love best by being loved by others and by living in a climate in which love prevails. In 1 Corinthians 13, the apostle Paul described several characteristics of love. These characteristics probably will be only words to a person who has not observed in someone else love suffering long, being kind, envying not, and not behaving itself improperly.

The fatherhood of God is one of the great doctrines of the Christian faith. Verbal explanation of this doctrine likely will mean little to a child whose physical father is domineering, vulgar, and abusive. The doctrine is learned best by one fortunate enough either to have or, in some other way, to be closely associated with a Christian father who exemplifies, in the manner possible on a human level, the great attributes of God the heavenly Father.

A major task of both the church and the Christian home is to provide an atmosphere in which God's eternal truths intersect the human needs of persons in normal and informal experiences. Selfishness and bickering in home or church can contradict and negate overt attempts to provide Christian training. On the other hand, an atmosphere of openness and love perhaps is the most effective teaching method a home or church can employ. Children, youth, and adults, in a profound way, demonstrate the truth of the book title: *They Learn What They Live.*[2]

2. Organized Church Groups

Although learning occurs in many ways outside organized learning groups, life-changing learning experiences can, and do, occur as persons participate in Bible classes and other learning groups which meet under the aegis of the church. If this were not true, millions of hours would be wasted each week as multitudes gather in church groups for study and discussion.

Structured learning is far too complex and elusive to be classified in a few self-contained categories. It can be said, however, that there are at least three general kinds of learning. They are inductive, deductive, and action/reflection.

No one kind is "best" as a constant pattern for a group. If the teacher or group leader keeps clearly in mind the lifelong learning task relevant to the curriculum unit, he or she might find it useful to try to induce all three kinds of learning from time to time.

In deductive learning, the group begins by exploring a Bible passage, a Christian doctrine, or some other reality in the Christian tradition. After identifying the central truth, group members seek to find in their daily lives either practical applications of the truth or the specific application of the truth to a particular situation. Some methods which frequently are useful in deductive teaching/learning are inquiry, lecture (used appropriately), question/answer, symposium, and panel discussion.

Inductive learning begins with specifics and moves to generalizations based on those specifics. In Christian education, the realities of the Christian faith are considered in reaching generalizations based on the specifics which are explored. Some methods which frequently are useful in inductive teaching/learning are case study, role playing, research report, and interview analysis.

Action/reflection combines components of both deductive and inductive learning in what may be described as a spiral learning curve. Steps, or phases, in action/reflection learning are (1) awareness, (2) exploration, (3) experimental action, (4) reflection, (5) reorientation, and (6) revised action, etc.

Action/reflection learning is especially prominent in the Christian Education/Shared Approaches curriculum plan. There also is an interesting similarity with the learning tasks identified in the Cooperative Curriculum Project as described in chapter 4.

An individual or group can enter the action/reflection cycle either at the point of studying a great reality of the Christian faith or at the point of focusing concern on a personal or social problem. If beginning with a reality of the Christian faith, such as the efficacy of prayer, the learner(s) would move successively into an exploration of biblical teachings on prayer, exploratory actions in praying, reflections on the results, reorientation in the light of further Bible study, and renewed (and, hopefully, improved) efforts to practice in their personal lives biblical teachings on prayer.

If the group members begin the action/reflection cycle at the point of concern over a personal or social problem, they would continue successively with an exploration of the problem, experimental actions to correct the problem, reflections of results in the light of Christian teachings, reorientation, revised action, etc.

It is unrealistic to assume that a complete action/reflection cycle can always be completed during a thirty-minute class session. In some cases, a teacher might (1) lead a group in an exploration during one class session; (2) suggest experimental action during the following days; (3) guide the group members in reflection and reorientation during the next class session; and (4) suggest further experimental action on an individual basis later.

Under other circumstances, the teacher might simply use one small segment of the action/reflection cycle in a class session. For example, after guiding the class in studying a particular truth, the teacher might suggest that class members take a few minutes to reflect on the implications of that truth in their personal lives.

The planning which a teacher does for a class session is a crucial step in relating the church's curriculum plan and the personal needs of class members. In the next chapter, the reader will find an explanation of steps which many teachers and other leaders have found helpful in preparing for teaching a Bible class and for guiding other church groups in discipleship training.

3. *Ministry*

Some of life's most valuable lessons are learned in direct service to persons in need. A person may have an intellectual knowledge of a truth without understanding its real meaning. Helping someone in need may cause that person to understand for the first time the real meaning of a truth which has been professed for years.

Compassion, for example, is a cardinal attribute of the Christian life. The Bible has a great deal to say about it. Perhaps the most familiar passage is the parable of the good Samaritan. Through this story Jesus sought to use the direct experience of one person to communicate to others what it really means to feel compassion for a person in dire circumstances. Formal study can help persons gain some understanding of compassion, but it is unlikely that they will learn to become truly compassionate persons until, with God's help, they have emulated the good Samaritan in their own lives.

Every church has in its own community and in adjoining communities scores of persons who are in need of Christian ministry. Sometimes the urgency of human need is concealed by such familiar terms as *poverty, affluence, unemployment, depressed areas, exclusive residential section, pornography, vice, culturally deprived, aristocracy, and alcoholism.* But when each of these terms is used, it applies to real people who may be experiencing critical needs.

Certainly, the desire to help persons who are experiencing these needs should be the chief factor which motivates any group to engage in ministry actions. However, the learning experiences of the helpers themselves frequently are more important than the assistance they give to persons they help.

The learning value of service activities may be greatly increased if participants have an opportunity to discuss their experiences in retrospect. If several persons in a class, for example, spend a day working together in a community center they will observe many different things. Many of their observations they will not fully understand. By discussing together their experiences, especially if a more experienced person is available to counsel them and help them to interpret their observations, they are able to learn much more from their ministry experience.

It is especially important that direct service opportunities be included in the Christian education of modern youth. The present generation of young people is demonstrating an unusual amount of concern for less fortunate people. This concern is highlighted in their response to short-term, volunteer mission service, projects in ghetto areas, and other service opportunities. If their Christian education is limited to classroom experiences, they may never comprehend the relationship of the Christian faith to service to humanity or be able to render maximum service to persons they are seeking to serve.

4. *Crises Experiences*

A Christian couple, who had been married for fifteen years, were overjoyed at the birth of their first child. Both the husband and wife loved children, and they had looked forward with great anticipation to the experience of parenthood.

A few days after their happy event, the doctor broke some news to them which turned their deepest joy into utter despair. Their baby was suffering from Down's syndrome (mongolism) and would never be able to live a normal life. For several weeks they were almost overcome with feelings of disappointment, anguish, and hostility. But gradually, with the loving help of a Sunday School teacher, the eternal truth of God's grace and assurance of strength intersected their feeling of despair. A passage which they had read many times came to have special meaning for them. It was, "My grace is sufficient for thee: for my strength is made perfect in weakness" (2 Cor. 12:9).

In their hour of greatest disappointment and anguish, God's promise of strength crossed their deepest need. As a result, they learned the reality of God's grace. Their disappointment was no less real, but they learned to live with their burden. They both accepted work with the preschoolers in their church, and over a period of years they made a valuable contribution to the young children in their church family.

Crises can be the most teachable moments of life. Such experiences as illness or the loss of a loved one force a person to recognize his own personal limitations. At such times, many people are susceptible to spiritual realities which explain, sustain, or give hope for the future. If the spiritual reality has meaning to the person and seems to speak to his human dilemma, the crisis can become a valuable learning experience.

Helping persons who are facing crises to discover spiritual realities which can sustain and give them hope for the future calls for considerable skill and Christian love. Under some circumstances, reading a Scripture passage may increase hostility. The wise Christian leader seeks, with the help of the Holy Spirit, to encourage and guide the person in despair to find in God's eternal truths the answers to his own problems. The way in which that encouragement and guidance is given is influenced considerably by the feelings, attitudes, and responses of the person to whom he is ministering.

5. *Interpersonal Relationships*

The familiar Chinese proverb that one picture is worth a thousand words has particular relevance in Christian education. Some of God's eternal truths are learned best when one sees and experiences these truths being exemplified in the lives of other people.

A college student, while driving under the influence of alcohol, sideswiped a ten-year-old boy riding a bicycle along the side of the road. The boy was rushed to a hospital where he remained in critical condition for many weeks. The student, when he realized what he had done, was overcome with anguish, fear, and a strong sense of guilt. His most dreaded and difficult experience was meeting the parents of the injured child. But that experience did not turn out at all like he expected it to. The parents, although deeply grieved over their son's condition, showed genuine concern for the student himself. In the relationship he developed with these Christian parents during the weeks which followed, the student learned the real meaning of forgiveness.

Many interpersonal relationships are on a feeling level which defies verbal explanation. The student, for example, could not explain verbally the forgiveness he experienced with the distraught parents. Neither could he have understood it had someone explained it to him. But he *felt* their forgiveness, and his feeling came more from their emotional reaction to him than from any single thing they said.

Words are inadequate to describe some of the great principles of life. The real meaning of these principles is learned only when they are experienced in relationship with someone else.

6. *Direct Encounter*

One of the great tenets of the Christian faith is the fact that each individual can have direct access to God. One does not have to approach the heavenly Father through an earthly representative. As a result of the atoning death of Jesus on the cross, one can go directly to the Father through Christ our intermediary.

Some of the most valuable lessons in the Christian life are learned in direct encounter with God through Christ. The reality of God's existence cannot be learned simply through logical reasoning and discussion. Although logical reasoning and discussion can help, one really learns the reality of God's existence through direct encounter with God himself.

The Bible contains many promises that God hears and answers prayer. A person may accept the validity of prayer on the basis of what others tell him about it or even what he reads in the Bible. But he can never learn the real meaning of prayer until he experiences direct communion with God in meaningful prayer experiences.

How Can a Church Induce Learning?

Since there are many avenues to learning, what are the major ways a church can induce learning in the lives of its members? In view of how learning takes place, four ways seem especially productive.

1. Create a Christian Climate

Basic to everything else a church can do in Christian education is the establishment of a warm Christian climate. The spiritual climate of the church sets the tone not only for Christian education but for everything else a church does.

When there is dissension in a church, the spirit of the fellowship contradicts and, in many cases, can negate positive teachings. It might be possible for a church torn in strife to accomplish something worthwhile through its teaching ministry, but it would be as difficult as pushing a car uphill with its brakes on. A squabble in a business meeting says more to the youth and children of the church about how Christians settle differences of opinion than anything Sunday School teachers can do or say on Sunday morning. Thus, a church teaches more by what it is than by what its leaders say.

A spirit of loving commitment to God is the soundest possible base for a program of Christian education in a church. When such a spirit exists, it influences learners unconsciously to want to "grow in grace, and in the knowledge of our Lord and Saviour Jesus Christ" (2 Peter 3:18).

A church that would engage seriously in Christian education also should cultivate a spirit of love and mutual concern for each member. When learners feel that they are loved, their resistance to change is reduced and they are able to enter learning experiences more freely and creatively. Moreover, through the emotional climate of the church they learn the meaning of love and how it can be expressed in other settings.

A church also can teach by the sense of divine mission it reflects in its corporate actions and in the spirit of its leaders. When church members feel that they are a part of a group aware of its divine purpose on earth, they participate more fully in activities designed to train for this divine mission.

2. Provide Competent Leaders

A second thing a church can do to induce learning is to select competent Christian leaders. Not only do such leaders help to establish the spiritual climate undergirding the ministry of Christian education but they also shape the course of Christian education in the church.

Earlier we saw that the context of Christian education is the life and work of the church. This means that Christian education should not be restricted to group experiences on Sunday, but it should penetrate every aspect of the life of the church both gathered and scattered. If this is done, teachers and other leaders must recognize their responsibility for stimulating and guiding learning experiences outside the classroom as well as inside. They must be alert to informal opportunities for helping persons recognize meaningful learning experiences in the home, in business, at school, during personal crises, and in all other normal life situations.

Finally, a church can teach by selecting leaders whose personal lives communicate the truths which the church would teach. Some of the most valuable learnings which come to church members come unconsciously as they observe the conduct of leaders who are supposed to be communicants of the Christian faith.

3. Offer a Balanced Curriculum

Although a church may induce learning in other ways besides through its formal curriculum, any study of church-inspired learning opportunities must, of course, give serious attention to learning which takes place within the structure of organized classes and other learning groups. Since most of this book deals with the church's formal curriculum, only brief attention will be given to it at this point.

Every church needs at least a two-pronged educational curriculum. It needs an effective Bible-teaching program and a strong program of discipleship training.

If the Bible is given its rightful place, the foundation of the church's educational ministry will be its Bible-teaching program. In Sunday School, major emphasis will be on exploring the truths of the Bible and their relationship to life. No attempt will be made to use the Scriptures to support preconceived personal viewpoints or simply to undergird causes, however worthy. The Bible will be allowed to speak for itself, and learners will be led to search honestly, with the help of the Holy Spirit, for the message which God is seeking to communicate through his Word.

As essential as Bible study is, however, no program of Christian education in a church is complete unless Bible study is augmented by discipleship training. Growing Christians need special training in ways to live and communicate the Christian faith in daily life. They need opportunities to explore the relevancy of the Christian faith to pressing problems in personal, family, community, and national life. They also need training in special skills for effective Christian service. Their discipleship training should include many service-related learning opportunities. Jesus, recognizing the importance of training, spent a great deal of his time training his disciples. No church can afford to do less for its members.

4. *Develop Concerned Christians*

Probably the most important thing a church can do to induce learning is to develop in its members concerns which cause them to have meaningful learning experiences wherever they go throughout the week.

One concern a church should seek to cultivate in its members is an honest desire to grow in the Christian life. When a person has this desire, every problem and obstacle he encounters during the week becomes a learning opportunity. Temptations to lose one's temper, for example, become occasions for experimenting with ways to remain calm when things go wrong. Personal crises become times for learning more about how God guides and sustains when trials come. When a person honestly desires to grow as a Christian, life every day is filled with unanticipated and unstructured opportunities to learn more about the relevancy of the Christian faith to daily experience.

Finally, a church can spawn many learning experiences by cultivating in its members a growing concern to express their faith in ministry to others. A person learns many things by attempting to render service to other people. One learns some things about the persons being helped that one would probably never learn in any other way. Developing skills in ministry can be helpful in future activities. One of the greatest things a person can learn is the joy and deep satisfaction one gains in ministering in Christ's name to persons in need.

Notes

1. Clarice M. Bowman, *Ways Youth Learn* (New York: Harper & Bros., 1952), p. 64.

2. Helen G. Trager and Marian Radke Yarrow, *They Learn What They Live* (New York: Harper & Bros., 1952).

7
Planning Teaching-Learning Sessions

What steps should one take in planning to lead a group of people in a formal learning experience? This is a matter of great importance to Sunday School teachers and leaders of other learning groups in churches. The procedure which each one follows in planning is an important factor in determining the success or failure of efforts to stimulate and guide group learning. If the procedure is faulty, the preparation may be inadequate regardless of the amount of time spent in study. If the right steps are taken, the amount of time necessary for successful planning can be significantly reduced.

Three elements should be of special concern to anyone making preparations to lead a church group in a learning experience. One is the area of study described in the church-approved curriculum materials. These curriculum materials represent a carefully developed curriculum plan and include helps prepared by some of the best minds in the denomination. Although the teacher or leader may supplement these with other printed helps, careful attention needs to be given to the basic curriculum materials themselves if individual sessions are properly related to a broader plan of study.

Along with a consideration of printed lesson materials, teachers or group leaders should have a continuing concern for the individuals in their classes or groups. They are persons with special interests, needs, concerns, prejudices, abilities, and potentialities. All of these are valuable data for anyone planning to lead these persons in a learning experience.

The third major area of consideration in planning is the nature of the interaction desired for the learner in the curriculum content area and how to stimulate and guide that interaction. (Remember the crossing point theory discussed earlier!) This leads to a consideration of the relevant lifelong learning task and continuing learning activities. A review of the related learning task and continuing learning activities can be an important step in selecting teaching/learning goals, methods, and other learning aids.

Thus the objective of the teacher or group leader is, with the help of the Holy Spirit, to involve learners in a study of the lesson content in such a way that they experience learning on their own. Learning, you recall, is not simply a mathematical process in which new facts are added to ones previously known. It is more like a chemical reaction in which two elements are brought together, a reaction takes place, and the result is different from what either element was before.

The nature of the curriculum and the character of the group influence the exact planning procedure. Sunday School teachers have in the Bible material to be studied a divine "given" not found in other kinds of study materials. Discerning the message which God is communicating through the Scripture material is an important step in their lesson preparation.

The character of the learning group also influences the planning process. The Sunday School teacher is the leader of the group and, therefore, is the central figure in the group process. In discipleship training, major emphasis is on training for performance, and the principle of shared leadership may prevail. In this kind of a group, one person may do most of the planning, but several group members exercise leadership responsibilities during various phases of a given session. All of these factors influence the planning process.

In view of these differences, two general approaches to planning for group learning are discernible. They are identifiable as steps in planning to teach the Bible and steps in planning for discipleship training.

Steps in Planning to Teach the Bible

Bible study is the central activity in Christian education. It is essential, therefore, that persons who teach the Bible plan carefully for their important responsibility. There are at least five steps in planning to teach the Bible.[1]

1. Master the Bible Material

The first step, quite logically, is to master the Scripture material to be taught. The teacher should begin his general preparation as soon as possible after he receives the teacher's quarterly containing the lessons for a new quarter. By reading over introductory materials and scanning the lesson titles and proposed objectives, one is able to get an overview of plans for the entire quarter. If the lessons are organized into units, unit objectives should be selected and unit activities planned before the teacher begins work on the first session.

Specific preparation for an individual session should begin as early in the week as possible. If the teacher begins early and studies a little each day, his subconscious mind is able to generate insights and ideas even while he is consciously engaged in other activities. Also, the teacher who begins lesson preparation early in the week usually finds illustrations and other teaching materials which would not have occurred to him had he waited until Saturday night to do all of his lesson planning.

The teacher who would master the Bible material needs to have and to use adequate Bible study aids. A Bible translation in modern language is a must. A good commentary, atlas, and concordance also are helpful resources. Of course, the teacher will make major use of the teacher's quarterly and other resources provided by his denomination.

The meaning of a Scripture passage can best be understood in the light of its total context. It is essential, therefore, that the teacher consider the total context of the Scripture lesson. He can begin to get an understanding of a passage by asking such questions as these: Who wrote this book? Why was it written? What circumstances and thought patterns of the day are reflected in the passage? What is the exact meaning of key words and phrases? What other biblical teachings need to be kept in mind as one interprets this particular passage?

A final step in mastering the Bible lesson is to seek to discover the real meanings which God is seeking to communicate through the passage. The teacher should allow the Bible to speak for itself rather than attempting to read into the passage meanings which support personal biases or pet ideas. Although the teacher should study the passage diligently, using the best Bible-study aids available, much time should be spent in prayer asking God to reveal the true meanings which should be communicated to the class members.

2. State the Central Truth

After mastering the Bible material, the teacher needs to state as clearly as possible the central truth which will be communicated to class members. Many passages contain several truths which would be of value to class members. Because of the brevity of the class session and the nature of the learning process, it is better to select the one truth which seems to be of greatest relevance to class members. It is far better to help class members learn one central truth well than to cover several truths without leading them to master any one of them.

It is helpful for the teacher to write down the central truth which seems most relevant to the needs of class members. For example, a central truth of the story of the baby Moses in the basket-boat might be stated in various ways, depending upon the age and interests of class members. A teacher of adult men might state as the central truth: When God has a task for a man, he sees to it that the man is spared and prepared for the undertaking. A teacher of young children might state it: We should be thankful for the loving care our mothers and fathers give us.

3. Consider the Needs of Learners

After stating the central truth, the next step the teacher should take is to consider class members' needs which are related to the central truth.

If the teacher is to succeed in relating the central truth to important needs of class members, more than a superficial knowledge of the class members is needed. The teacher needs to know their deeper needs, aspirations, problems, and the circumstances of their day-by-day lives. These things simply cannot be learned through association with class members at church on Sunday. Personal relationships must be developed and maintained with them during the week. This is not always easy, and in some cases it may seem impossible. A teacher's work may allow little time during the week for association with members of the Sunday School class. Moveover, class members, who also have limited free time, may live in widely separated sections of a city. Nevertheless, the teacher should recognize the need for personal acquaintance and friendship with each class member, and should use to the best advantage each opportunity to cultivate this friendship.

Part of the answer to the problem of limited time for association with class members is for the teacher to develop skill in establishing and maintaining rapport with class members, even during the little time given to be with them. An observant teacher who relates well to other persons can learn more during a few brief contacts with a class member than another teacher might learn during more sustained contacts.

By talking with the pastor and others who know the class members, the teacher can gain additional valuable information about the needs and interests of those taught. Sometimes a perceptive and concerned class member can be a valuable source of information to the teacher.

Whatever plan the teacher has of becoming familiar with the personal needs of the class members, an important step in lesson preparation is to identify specific needs and possible attitudes relevant to the central truth of the lesson passage. This step in preparation is crucial if the teacher is successful on Sunday morning in relating the lesson to life.

4. Select an Aim

Ideally, because of the great differences in the needs of individual class members, the teacher would have a different aim for each class member. Since this does not seem feasible, it is important most of the time that an aim is chosen which expresses a need of the majority of the class members. It may be desirable under some exceptional circumstances, however, to select an aim related primarily to one or to only a few persons in the class.

The aim should be stated in terms of the desired response of the class members to the central truth of the Bible material. It should be definite, worthy, and reasonably attainable in the time allotted for formal teaching plus any follow-through activities which are planned. It should specify what the teacher hopes the class members will come to know, feel, or do, as a result of their exploration of the central truth of the lesson.

"Forgiveness Through the Cross" was the title of one lesson for adults. The Scripture passage was Luke 23:33-46. A possible aim for the teaching of that passage might be: to help class members, through guided study of Luke's account of the crucifixion, to face personally and realistically the question, What does the death of Jesus mean to me? This aim, although specific, is broad enough to relate to a wide range of problems in the lives of various members of a class. To one non-Christian, the main question might be the need for salvation and the way in which salvation is available through Christ's death on the cross. To a nominal Christian in the class, the meaning might be a challenge to recognize the significance of the Christian faith to daily life. To a warmhearted Christian in the class, the meaning might be added assurance of Christ's love and devotion.

A clearly stated aim is a valuable aid to the teacher in inducing learning by class members. Thus, selecting and clarifying a worthy aim is a great help to the teacher later in developing a lesson plan for guiding his class in a meaningful experience.

5. Develop a Teaching Plan

A teaching plan is not an outline of Bible material. It is a description of the steps a teacher proposes to take in involving class members in a meaningful study of the Scripture lesson and in applying the central truth of the lesson to their personal lives.

Although there are several general approaches which can be taken in accomplishing these objectives, there are three essential phases which should be included in every Bible-teaching lesson plan.

The first, of course, is a definite plan to attract the attention of the class members. In some highly motivated groups, it may be satisfactory to begin with a study of the Bible passage itself. Normally, however, it is good to find some other plan for gaining attention. The technique used to gain attention should be one which motivates interest in meaningful Bible study. A teacher could attract attention by doing a handstand or by relating a fascinating personal experience, but these would be poor introductions unless, somehow, they motivated interest in Bible study.

Another section of the lesson plan includes methods the teacher proposes to use in guiding the class in purposeful Bible study. The teacher makes a mistake by simply *telling* the class about the Bible lesson. It is far better to select methods and activities which will help members to discover for themselves what the Bible is saying. This may be done in several ways. One way is to raise a provocative question and suggest that members search the Scripture lesson for an answer. Although factual questions can lead to helpful Bible study, normally it is better for the central question the teacher raises to be one which will turn the class members to the Bible in search for a basic principle or meaningful truth. There are other techniques a teacher can use in guiding class members in purposeful Bible study, and the skillful teacher uses varying approaches from time to time.

One of the most important steps in developing a lesson plan is to decide upon ways to help members discover the relevance of the central truth of the Bible lesson to their daily life experiences. Simply telling them may not be sufficient—even if, indeed, the teacher always knew the most meaningful application of Bible truths to the lives of class members. The skillful teacher uses appropriate methods to help class members discover these applications for themselves.

The final step in developing plans for teaching many lessons is to identify suggestions which can be made to class members for putting the central truth of the lesson into practice. Follow-through activities like these are valuable aspects of the learning experience.

Steps in Planning for Discipleship Training

Churches of several denominations have groups organized to provide special training in church membership and Christian discipleship. One of the outstanding movements of this kind since the turn of the century has been the

Church Training (Training Union) movement in Southern Baptist churches. Missionary organizations and music programs also provide discipleship training. Sometimes this work is limited to youth fellowship groups. In other cases, it includes provisions for other age groups also.

Two features usually characterize this kind of training. The first is a strong emphasis on acquiring understandings, attitudes, and skills needed for specific types of Christian service. Another is a strong emphasis on the learning group. Although there usually is an elected leader who is primarily responsible for advanced planning, there is recognition of the dynamics of the group and an emphasis on shared leadership during group sessions.

Planning for a group learning experience in a setting like this calls for steps somewhat different from those followed by a Sunday School teacher who is planning to teach a Bible lesson. Many group leaders have found five steps to be especially appropriate.

1. Cultivate the Climate

The emotional climate of the learning group is a highly important factor in learning. When group members are experiencing discouragement, apathy, or indifference, it is highly unlikely that the learning experience will be successful. On the other hand, if the group members are highly motivated to investigate the area to be studied, some meaningful learning is almost certain to take place.

There are several things a group leader can do prior to the session to begin to cultivate a climate for learning. Involving group members in the planning process is one highly effective way. Advance publicity, designed to stimulate interest in the area to be explored, contributes to a stimulating learning environment. Even an enthusiastic attitude by the leader in inviting members to the group can help to create a feeling of expectancy.

The physical condition and arrangements of the room in which the group meets contribute to the learning climate. Proper lighting, a comfortable temperature, and isolation from outside noises are highly important. An orderly arrangement of chairs and other room furniture helps to set the stage for learning. All of these matters should be given serious attention prior to the time group members begin to arrive.

The initial experience a learner has on entering the room in which the study is to be conducted is important. If he is made to feel welcome and a part of the group, he is much more likely to participate freely in the group study. Thus, an important aspect of advance planning is the making of necessary arrangements to welcome members and create a feeling of friendliness in presession conversations.

Finally, the way in which the group study or discussion is initiated is an extremely important factor in creating a climate for learning. Normally a group leader should attempt to do two things in introducing a topic for discussion. First, the leader should seek to stimulate interest in and a sense of direction or purpose to the study. If the leader can succeed during the first few minutes to stimulate interest in exploring a particular problem, some learning is almost certain to take place.

Also, plans should be made to relate the session topic to the unit theme early in the discussion period. Most curriculum materials are organized into units of study. A unit is a series of closely related learning plans designed to help persons gain increased understanding of or proficiency in a particular area of study. Although a unit might be dealt with in one session, normally several sessions are devoted to a single unit of study.

Thus, one of the first steps a leader takes in the specific planning for an individual session is to consider the relationship of the session to the unit of which it is a part. The particular location of the session in the unit is an important clue. If it is the introductory session, the group leader may want to major on orientation, motivation, previewing plans, and helping the group set learning goals and plan activities for the unit. If the session concludes a unit of study, the leader may want to place major emphasis on helping group members reach and/or test decisions growing out of the study. Emphasis during intermediate sessions may be on helping the group to acquire understandings, develop attitudes, or acquire skills relevant to the general objective of the unit. Planning for any session should include the development or use of some technique for helping the group understand the relationship of the session to its unit.

2. *Select a Learning Goal*

No group ever engages in completely aimless study or discussion. Unfortunately, however, the aim of many groups is simply "to have a program." In most such cases, the outcome is a period of time spent in unprofitable discussion.

Thus, the second step a leader should take in planning for group learning is to identify a specific goal for the session. Although the goal later may be altered by the group, skillful group leaders recognize the need for selecting at least a tentative learning goal to serve as a guide in their planning.

The theme for study provides a clue to a desirable goal, but it is no more than a clue. Even when the printed materials contain a suggested goal, that goal should not be accepted unless it represents a real need of the group members.

Any particular study theme can suggest several possible goals. The specific goal a leader selects should be determined in the light of the needs and interests of members of the group. Suppose, for example, the theme of study suggested in the quarterly is "Recognizing Symptoms of Alcoholism." The obvious learning goal would be to help group members learn to detect these symptoms in the lives of acquaintances, friends, or loved ones. However, inherent in the session content are several other possible learning goals. (Content, you recall, is basic realities and experiences with those realities.) Thus the basic content for the session is alcoholics and alcoholism. Other possible goals in exploring this basic content might be: (1) to investigate and evaluate resources in our community for helping alcoholics, (2) to learn a few general principles for working with alcoholics, (3) to discover some of the causes of alcoholism, and (4) to investigate the influence of alcoholism in our community.

If, in the light of the particular interests or needs of group members, the leader selects a learning goal other than the one proposed in the quarterly, it may be necessary to look elsewhere for most of the resources to be used in the group exploration. However, the extra effort made necessary by the new learning goal is worthwhile if it better meets the needs of group members.

Often it is well to rephrase the goal as a provocative problem. Goals stated as problems are much more likely to induce interest and discussion on the part of group members. The possible goals stated earlier might be restated, for example: What are the resources in our community for ministering to alcoholics and how effective are they in their ministry? What are some general principles for working with alcoholics? What are some causes of alcoholism? What is the influence of alcoholism in our community?

Any one of these questions could be used to stimulate provocative study and discussion.

3. Plan Learning Activities

Learning is an active process. Although listening can be active, and meaningful learning sometimes takes place as one listens to a lecture, it is unlikely that learning will continue if the lecture is the only method used or if the lecture is used when another method would have been more appropriate. After selecting a learning goal, the next step a leader takes, therefore, is to select methods which will cause the group to move toward the achievement of the goal.

Learning methods are tools. Like other tools, they are designed to accomplish specific objectives. If used properly, they can be very useful. If used improperly, they will produce little, if any, worthwhile results.

The topic for discussion proposed in one quarterly was "Strangers in Our Midst." The resource material described many of the needs of internationals enrolled in the colleges and universities in this country. A leader using the discussion material might plan a symposium with several group members discussing in sequence the needs described in the quarterly.

If the group members decided, instead, to focus on undocumented aliens in their own city, the best approach might be for the leader to make advance assignments to group members to do research on the problems of the undocumented aliens and report back to the group when it meets to discuss the problem.

Developing sensitivity to the needs of internationals in their city might be still another worthy goal. Two good methods to achieve this goal would be to encourage members to tell of the needs of particular internationals they know and to lead the group in case studies of foreign language-speaking people in their own community.

If the learning goal were to lead members to discover ways their church could minister to internationals in its community, a study of what other churches are doing would be one possible method. Another method would be to investigate many of the needs of the foreign-language-speaking people and discuss ways the church could meet many of these needs.

The chart appearing later in this chapter specifies several methods which usually are effective means of reaching certain worthwhile goals.

When formal group study is supplemented by related activities outside the group, lasting learning is more likely to take place. One of the simplest outside activities a leader can propose is the suggestion that group members seek in their normal daily experiences examples of the principle or conditions being studied. For example, if the topic being discussed is prejudice, the leader might suggest at the close of the session that group members be on the alert during the week for examples of prejudice and to analyze the results of what they see.

Experimental behavior is another type of follow-through activity. If, for example, the group is studying Christian responses to temptation, the leader might suggest that group members be on the alert for personal temptations during the coming week and, when they do face temptation, test the responses considered by the group during the discussion.

Another valuable follow-through activity is to recommend the reading of books or magazine articles related to the theme of group study. One group leader frequently reviews half of a book or article to the group and encourages them to finish reading it themselves. Out of curiosity to discover the remainder of the book or article, many group members do the reading who would never have done it otherwise.

Group or individual projects also can be meaningful learning experiences. A mission action, related to the study content and initiated at the beginning of a unit, can be an extremely valuable aid to the learning during the study of a unit.

A METHODS GUIDE FOR GROUP LEADERS

If your learning goal is to help your group:	*Good methods for use are:*
1. Gain a better understanding of facts, plans, conditions, or areas of content	Lecture, symposium, investigation, and report
2. Identify, explore, or analyze a problem of mutual interest to the group with no thought of reaching a group decision for formal action	Panel discussion, dialogue, colloquy
3. Identify, explore, or analyze a problem for the purpose of reaching a group decision for later action by the group or by individuals in the group	Group problem solving (formal group discussion)
4. Analyze and evaluate conflicting viewpoints	Debate, panel discussion
5. Develop personal skill in dealing with problem situations	Role playing, case study

4. Prepare Learning Aids

God endowed most people with five senses. These senses are receptacles of stimuli which aid learning. The more of the senses which are involved in a learning activity the more likely learning is to take place.

After determining what methods will be used, the group leader's next step is to plan learning aids to augment the spoken word. In planning learning aids, the wise leader seeks to utilize meaningfully more than one of the five senses of his group members.

The chalkboard has been a popular aid to learning through the years. If the leader expects to use the chalkboard, plans when to use it and how to use it need to be made. It is a good idea, also, to check in advance to be certain chalk and eraser are available.

Newsprint charts also are popular learning aids. One advantage of the newsprint chart over the chalkboard is that it can be prepared in advance and transported easily to the meeting place, thus avoiding the necessity for the leader's reaching the meeting place in time to print an outline on the chalkboard. Although newsprint and Magic Markers are easily available, a suitable substitute, if neither is available, is the classified ad section of the newspaper and black liquid shoe polish. The dauber in the shoe polish makes an excellent printing instrument.

The cassette tape recorder can be used in producing valuable learning aids. Civic or religious leaders in the community can be interviewed during the week and their voices brought via tape into the learning group at the church. With a little imagination, group leaders can find many other ways to introduce outside personalities into their learning groups via the tape recorder.

Pictures and curios offer additional possibilities. Pictures illustrating persons or conditions being studied and discussed can make the learning experience much more realistic. Curios add color and emotional tone to the learning experience.

Other learning aids which enrich study and discussion include the overhead projector, the flannelboard, the record player, filmstrips and filmclips, the opaque projector, graphs, posters, "hidden voices," flipcharts, and motion pictures.

Two cautions should be considered by the group leader who plans to use learning aids. First, be certain that the learning aid is an aid and not an ornament. It is possible for a learning aid to attract so much attention to itself that it obscures rather than illuminates the point it is intended to illustrate. Another caution to the group leader is to carefully check the aid in advance to be certain that it is in working order. Many potential learning experiences have been sabotaged by a contrary projector.

5. *Evaluate the Results*

No learning session is complete until it has been evaluated. Every session should be evaluated by the leader. The group itself should be involved occasionally in evaluation.

Armchair evaluation is a form available to every leader. It can be conducted by raising and thinking through such questions as these: To what extent did I accomplish my objective? How effective were the methods used? Did the learning aids accomplish their purposes? Were there any problems which prevented the group from full participation? How did I perform as a leader?

The PMR, or post meeting reaction, is a useful tool for involving the entire group in the evaluation. In this plan, the entire group is involved immediately after the close of a session in an evaluation of their group experience.

The process observer is another useful plan. In this plan, one person appointed in advance observes the processes of the group and reports later to the leader or to the entire group. Although a process observer may observe and report on any aspect of the group discussion, normally he or she concentrates on parts of the discussion which obstructed the group or helped it to move toward its objectives.

Note

1. For a more detailed treatment of these steps, see Howard P. Colson, *Preparing to Teach the Bible* (Nashville: Convention Press, 1959).

8
The Bible in the Curriculum

In Christian education we begin with the Bible as the divine "given." It is the basis of all our curriculum. Without it there would be no Christian teaching. The Bible is the indispensable book.[1] There are, however, a number of important questions about the Bible's relation to Christian education which need to be raised and answered. This chapter will deal with those questions.

What Is the Nature of the Bible?

1. *The Bible is the record of God's self-revelation.*—It presents a gradual and progressive unfolding of his persistent purpose to communicate to men a knowledge of himself and his will for them. It is an account not only of his mighty words but of his mighty acts on behalf of men. Before Christ came, the greatest of his mighty acts was the deliverance of the enslaved Hebrews from their bitter bondage in Egypt. But the greatest of all his mighty acts was the Christ event; that brought to a climax the long years of the unfolding of God's redeeming love. Because the Bible is the record of God's self-revelation with its consummation in Jesus Christ, it is the indispensable foundation for all Christian teaching.

2. *The Bible is the repository of God's redemptive message for the world.*— It contains the gospel, the good news of salvation; and, as Sara Little has written, the curriculum of true Christian education is a "gospel-centered curriculum."[2] Without the Bible, the message of redemption would either have been lost or have become woefully distorted.

3. *The Bible is inspired by God.*—In its pages we read that "all scripture is inspired by God" (2 Tim. 3:16, RSV) and that in the production of it "men moved by the Holy Spirit spoke from God" (2 Peter 1:21, RSV). One of the unique things about the Bible is that it presents truth which our unaided human intelligence could never have discovered. Looking at the Bible from that stand-

point we have feelings akin to those of Peter when, in a tense and critical hour, he said to Jesus, "Lord, to whom shall we go? You have the words of eternal life" (John 6:68, RSV).

4. *The Bible has been providentially preserved.*—We have it today in trustworthy form, in translations which accurately and clearly convey its message to common people. We must not overlook or disparage the painstaking labors of copyists and translators in this process. They deserve much credit, especially since the Scriptures have had bitter foes through the years who would like to have seen the sacred writings distorted or altogether obliterated. But to persons of Christian faith it is plain that God himself has presided over the process by which his Word was preserved and translated so that we might have it today.

5. *The Bible is God's gift to his church.*—As James D. Smart observes,

> It is the record of the Word of God that created the Church, and that is able to create the Church ever afresh when it is rightly heard and obeyed. Thus the Word of God and the Church are inseparable. Both are necessary to God that he may reveal himself in judgment and in mercy as the God that he is. Word and Church belong together, and in no other order than that—the Word first and the Church second. The Word creates the Church, not the Church the Word. The Church is wholly dependent upon the Word, and has no existence without it.[3]

6. *The Bible furnishes the only authoritative guidance for Christian life and work.*—This, of course, is strictly an evangelical viewpoint. The Roman Catholic Church holds that the Bible and the church are together the rule of faith and conduct, with the church sometimes given priority over the Bible. But evangelical Christians hold that the Bible alone is the norm. If, then, the Bible is the norm, how shall its guidance, its standards, its principles, and its precepts become operative in the lives of persons except through the teaching ministry?

7. *The Bible brings men to Christ.*—As Rolston well said, "The Bible is the indispensable book because it is the effective instrument through which the living Lord is continually calling men and women into fellowship with him as Lord and Saviour."[4]

What Is the Place of the Bible in Curriculum?

1. *The Bible is the source of Christian teaching.*—"Most Christian educators are convinced that the Bible must be presented as the Word of God so that the

pupil will know that it is intended to speak to him."[5] But if the Bible is to be the means by which God speaks to the learner, the learner must be taught its content. This does not mean that he must know it in its entirety before God can speak to him. The fact is, God often speaks to those who use his Word at a very early stage of their exposure to its message. But always, when God speaks to learners by means of the Bible, it is on the basis of some portion of its content. That is why we are concerned to give our pupils exposure to the Bible itself. By studying the narratives, poems, sermons, laws, precepts, Gospels, and apocalypses, they will come to hear the voice of God speaking to them and will be challenged to make a personal response in terms of faith, love, and obedience.

2. *The Bible is the norm for Christian teaching.*—At the heart of evangelical faith is the conviction that all Christian teaching must be judged in the light of the Scriptures.

The Bible has been the basis of Christian teaching in all eras of the church's history when evangelical faith flourished at its best. Luther's famous slogan *sola scriptura* epitomizes this high regard for the written Word of God. By the time of Luther, the main body of Christendom had moved so far from its divine origin that heresy after hersey had appeared. It was necessary, therefore, to find some basis for disinguishing between the true and the false in the teaching that was prevalent. What could the criterion be but the Bible? This was what Luther contended for at the Diet of Worms: "Unless I am convinced by Scripture and plain reason—I do not accept the authority of popes and councils, for they have contradicted each other—my conscience is captive to the Word of God. I cannot and I will not recant anything, for to go against conscience is neither right nor safe. God help me. Amen."[6]

3. *The Bible is the instrument for Christian teaching.*—It is our chief tool in the teaching process. The Holy Spirit uses the Word to bring persons to conviction and conversion and to help them grow in grace toward the goal of full Christian maturity. The New Testament was written that men might believe that Jesus is the Christ, the Son of God, and that believing they may have life in his name (John 20:31). "All Scripture . . . is useful for teaching the truth, rebuking error, correcting faults, and giving instruction for right living" (2 Tim. 3:16, TEV).

Is the Bible Relevant?

As people read the Bible seeking the guidance of the Holy Spirit, they find authentic and conclusive answers to their deepest and most urgent questions, such as, Who is God? How may I know him? What does he expect of me? The Bible speaks with relevance to the needs of humanity because it is the eternal God, our contemporary, who speaks through it. There is no higher authority to which we can turn for knowledge of God and his will. The same God who spoke through faithful men of old and inspired those who wrote is present in the person of the Holy Spirit to speak through the Scriptures today to those who seek to hear him. Just as God inspired men of old to write the Bible, so today he enlightens the reader of the Bible in his search for truth.

The Bible deals vitally and authentically with humanity's persistent life needs. And as was pointed out in chapter 6, it is at the point where an eternal reality of the gospel intersects with a persistent life need of the learner that true Christian learning takes place. In such learning needs are met, and a person is changed. Such is the relevance of biblical truth. For example, when a person learns and accepts God's changeless and seeking love, supremely manifested in Jesus Christ, that person's persistent need for reconciliation, meaning, acceptance, integrity, security, and freedom are adequately met, and his alienation from God is overcome.[7] Or take the persistent need for personal significance and for a richly satisfying life. This need is met as a person discovers and appropriates the teachings of the Scriptures concerning the Christian relationship of faith, love, and obedience toward God, and the corollary teachings about love for one's fellowmen.[8]

The relevance of the Bible to human need means that the curriculum of Christian education must be so planned as to give the best possible opportunity for the Holy Spirit to use the Bible in the lives of learners, so that through this means the living God will confront them and give them the opportunity of responding in faith, love, and obedience.

What Is the Authority of the Bible?

The basis for the claim that the Bible is spiritually authoritative is the fact that it came from God. But more must be said than that, for the Bible is not some automatic machine grinding out glib answers to difficult questions. It is a dynamic and vital book whose authority resides not in mere words but in the divine truth which the words set forth.

Proof-texting is in no sense the best way to use the Bible in Christian education, but that is not to say that the words of Scripture are unimportant. As a matter of fact, there *is* power in the words themselves, as every devout believer has experienced. Yet the words are but the conveyors of the truth, and the truth is the important thing. That is why no single translation of the Bible has any superior claim to sanctity. The best translation is the one which most accurately and clearly sets forth the meanings which the original writers intended to convey. The words of the Bible are means to an end, and the end is the truth which God has revealed. That truth is the authority we seek.

On the one hand we may say that the Bible is authoritative because the truths it reveals have their source in God. On the other hand, we may say that God has revealed the things we find in the Bible because they are true, and that fact is what gives them their authority. Certainly the nature of the truth set forth in the Scriptures is such that the honest reader realizes that it could never have come from any merely human source.

Our task is not to argue for the authority of the Bible, nor to try to force that authority on unwilling persons. Rather, it is to help make the biblical message clear and appealing, so that our learners may discover its authority for themselves. If this is to come about, curriculum materials must be planned with genuine respect for the authority of Scripture. And likewise in the local church, teachers and leaders need to reflect with sincerity and dedication their acceptance of that authority.

Does the Bible Have Power Today?

The Bible has power to affect individuals and groups. When persons respond to its message, they become changed individuals. They come to know God, and they discover the true meaning of life: indeed, they receive life itself and find trustworthy, satisfying guidance for this present world and hope for the world to come. Every genuine Christian is a living testimony to the transforming power of biblical truth.

The power of the Bible is also manifested in the life and work of churches. From New Testament days until the present, whenever a church has seriously taken biblical truth as its authority and earnestly sought to put the truth into practice, that church has been marked by vitality and power; it has made its presence felt for the blessing of its own members, for the good of its community, and for the uplift of humanity at large.

Bible teaching can help solve the great problems of society. The biblical revelation bears vitally on such matters as human rights and human relations. It offers the clue as to how human beings should deal with race relations, industrial relations, problems of capital and labor, the family, international relations, war and peace. Its teaching concerning the infinite worth of the individual lies at the basis of all it has to say or imply about such questions. If the churches had done a better job of teaching the biblical revelation, the world would be in a far better moral and social condition today.

Prejudices and animosities are difficult to overcome. In many instances the only cure is the transformation of thought and life that comes through personal regeneration and the sanctifying work of the Holy Spirit in believing hearts. Curriculum planners and Christian educators meet a challenge at this point. They must do everything in their power to bring the message of the Bible to bear on every aspect of life.

How Can We Use the Bible with Integrity?

If the Bible is to be used with integrity, it is essential that we recognize its nature as both human and divine. We have emphasized the fact that it is divine. But it is human also. It was written by human beings, who, though inspired, were permitted to express themselves in their own individual ways. The idea of a divinely dictated Bible is not what is meant by inspiration. Peter did not write like Paul, nor did Ezekiel write like Isaiah. We miss a very important consideration if we overlook the human elements in the Bible.

Again, the Bible must be interpreted in accordance with the progressive nature of the revelation it records. God had to begin with his people where they were; he had to deal with them according to the level of spiritual development which they had achieved. That is why so much of the Old Testament stands on a lower moral and spiritual plane than the New Testament. Divine revelation moved upward toward its climax in Jesus Christ. We therefore have no right to expect that the Old Testament, which was preparatory to the coming of Christ, should measure up to the high spiritual level of the matchless Son of God. Much that is in the Old Testament is sub-Christian simply because it was pre-Christian. This fact can never be overlooked in an honest interpretation of the Old Testament. This is not to say that the Old Testament is unimportant. It is vastly important, but it has to be dealt with for what it is, as preparation for Christ and not as the full and final revelation of God. If the Old Testament by itself were adequate as a revelation of God, Christ would never have needed to come.

Furthermore, the Bible contains a variety of literary forms. These include legislation, poetry, drama, history, preaching, parable, letters, and apocalyptic writings. Each of these must be interpreted in keeping with its character. Parable is not history, and law is not gospel; poetry is not always to be taken literally, nor are precepts to be explained away by taking them figuratively.

If we are to use the Bible with integrity, we must take advantage of the results of sound scholarship and the best of critical interpretation. These are not something to be feared; they are means which God uses to help men get at the true meaning of his Word.

Moreover, the biblical revelation must always be used in keeping with its spiritual purpose. In some instances that purpose is apparent; in others it lies hidden and has to be dug for. But the basic principle to be observed is that the Bible is a religious book, a book about God, his nature, his will, and his mighty works for human benefit; it is not a book of science. There are many questions which the Bible makes no attempt to answer. The reason is that these questions lie outside its purpose.

The areas of content with which the Bible deals may be summarized in the following categories: Life and Its Setting: the Meaning and Experience of Existence; Revelation: the Meaning and Experience of Redemption; Vocation: the Meaning and Experience of Discipleship; The Church: the Meaning and Experience of Christian Community.[9]

How Shall We Interpret the Bible?[10]

An essential part of designing Christian education curriculum involves the application of the best results of the science of biblical hermeneutics. Hermeneutics has to do with the principles of interpretation. The following principles are recognized and observed by all sound Bible scholars.[11]

1. First of all, *every individual has the right to come to the Bible for himself.* It is his privilege, under God, to exercise his own divinely given competence to explore the Bible, discover its meaning, and appropriate that meaning to his own life. This is not to say that he will disregard the spiritual, scholarly efforts of others to discover God's meaning, but he will not be a slave to their opinions, nor will he be satisfied to let others do his thinking for him.

2. *The first question that must be answered about any text is, What does it say?* The students must never try to read into a passage what is not there. They must not try to make it say what they would like for it to say or what they think it ought to say. The question is, Exactly what does it say? In order to answer that question, all the resources of linguistic and historical study need to be drawn

upon. Here is where lexicons, grammars, and scholarly commentaries are called for. Here, also, is where recent versions can be very helpful.

3. Another consideration is *whether the passage is to be taken literally or figuratively.* Usually this has to be determined in accordance with the type of writing one is dealing with. To interpret figurative language literally can be tragically misleading. The opposite error may be equally tragic.

4. Still another question to be faced is this: *Does the passage present a permanent and universal truth or is it only local and temporary?* The dietary regulations of the Mosaic code are an example of the latter, as is also Paul's word to the women in Corinth about keeping silent in church.

In all interpretation of Scripture it is necessary to get beyond the words to the ideas and truths for which they stand. Of course, one must first understand what the words say. But beyond the words is the truth, and the truth is the main consideration.

5. *When dealing with narrative portions, the interpreter must recognize that beyond the event lies the witness of believers to the meaning of the event.* Thus the Exodus of Israel from Egypt was more than the migration of a band of slaves; it was a mighty act of God by which he sublimely demonstrated his steadfast love and redeeming grace. Similarly, the Gospel of John does more than tell the story of some of Jesus' activities. It goes on to interpret the spiritual meaning of those activities.

6. Always in dealing with a portion of Scripture, whether long or short, it is important to ask, *What is the central message of the passage?* Otherwise one can get lost in peripheral details and miss the main point. This can be particularly true in the case of the parables.

7. Another important principle is to *interpret Scripture by means of Scripture.* For example, difficult or obscure passages should be understood in the light of passages in which the meaning is clear. There is a divine unity about the Bible which comes from the fact that its writers were all moved by one Spirit. In seeking to understand the meaning of any particular passage, we should seek to interpret it in the light of the Bible's message as a whole.

8. And then we should *examine the findings of the best biblical scholars, ancient and modern.* Through the better commentaries we can learn how a passage has been understood by serious students through the ages, and this can keep us from going too far afield from the consensus of Christian thought.

9. A final principle is *the recognition that Jesus Christ is the Lord of the Scriptures.* This means that any interpretation that disagrees with his teaching

cannot be right. His authority as the Son of God is supreme. "The norm by which Scripture . . . is to be judged is the mind and heart of the Lord Jesus Christ as he is witnessed to in the New Testament."[12]

How Shall We Use the Bible with Children?

The use of the Bible with children is a subject calling for special attention. The Bible was not written for children; it was written for adults. When it is used with children it requires unusually wise handling, a point which has often been overlooked or disregarded by some well-intentioned persons. There is no telling what harm has been wrought by the assumption that children have a natural readiness for almost any part of the Bible, especially the narrative portions, and that it is the duty of teachers to give them as much Bible as possible at the earliest possible age. The fact is, children do not have a natural readiness for all portions of the Bible. Who would think of subjecting a first, second, or third-grader to the disciplines of calculus, organic chemistry, nuclear physics, or the history of Afghanistan? Everyone knows that years of preparatory studies in arithmetic, general science, and history are necessary before students are ready for the more advanced and difficult courses. Similarly it takes years of preparation and of personal and social development before children are ready for some of the things in the Bible which adults are capable of dealing with.

One of the main cautions to be observed in the use of the Bible with younger age groups is to avoid teaching them anything from or about the Scriptures which they will later have to unlearn. Well-intentioned, but overzealous teachers are sometimes guilty of treating children as if they were miniature adults—which they certainly are not. Those who design curriculum plans involving the use of the Bible with children need to be well acquainted both with the Bible and with child nature. These two factors must be in proper relationship or much harm can be done to child life. The mere fact that the Bible is "taught" to little boys and girls does not guarantee sound spiritual results. It can be taught in ways that will give children twisted concepts, in ways that will instill fear instead of trust, in ways that will generate a dislike for spiritual things instead of love. All such mistakes are to be zealously avoided.

When these matters are appropriately taken into consideration, however, it is possible to use the Bible very effectively with children. In fact, all of the great themes of the Bible can be communicated to them when it is done in keeping with their present stage of development. Lewis J. Sherrill states that "each theme of revelation probably is relevant ultimately to every age in the life span'' and that a theme ''can be communicated non-verbally from the earliest days of life, then communicated both verbally and symbolically as age advances.''[13] And Randolph Crump Miller in his *Biblical Theology and Christian Education*[14] makes the point that the way to do this communicating with the growing youngster is to do it in terms of the normal life relationships which the child naturally understands and appreciates. One application of Miller's principle is that the child must be able to identify appropriately with a biblical character or biblical situation, or he will learn either nothing or something equivalent to a distortion of the biblical truth.

As to which Bible stories are appropriate for children, there is considerable diversity of opinion even among children's workers themselves. There are extremists who go so far as to limit the total number of usable stories to a very few. On the other hand there are those who think that almost any story is appropriate. Neither view is really tenable.

Certainly the idea that the Bible cannot be taught at all levels is false. The basic question is not when, but how. And here is where wise curriculum planners and skillful teachers come into play. In the hands of the right kind of teacher the Bible can be most effectively used with children. Such a teacher becomes the living embodiment of the truth, and thus the Bible becomes meaningful and powerful in the child's life.

Smart has written some very significant statements concerning this whole matter.

> Grading . . . is a necessity in the use of the Bible, but grading does not mean perversion of the Bible in order to get something remotely resembling it that can be used with young children. Grading simply means that we do not try to make the child take any step in his pilgrimage into the Bible until he is ready for it. It requires an abandonment of the attitude that the child will be benefitted by the mere quantity of the Bible with which he is familiar. The purpose of instructing the child in the Scriptures is not just that he may know the Scriptures, but that he may have faith in God as he is revealed in the Scriptures. The quantity of Scripture known is irrelevant, for one passage, rightly heard and understood, may open the way to faith, while a hundred passages which have no definite meaning for the child's life may produce only confusion.[15]

Let the Bible "Come Alive"

In the curriculum of Christian education every honest effort should be made to apply the Bible faithfully to contemporary life. Unfortunately, some Sunday School teachers seem to ignore this principle altogether. They seem content to present biblical content as if it had nothing to do with the life of their pupils in today's world. Such teaching is little more than the teaching of history or literature, whereas the purpose of Christian education is to lead learners to have encounters with God that will transform their lives.

Another unfortunate fact is that oftentimes unworthy or false applications of the biblical message are made. In such cases the true message of the passage is missed. In some instances this is the result of ignorance; in others it represents prejudice, or the desire to make the Bible say what persons want it to say instead of what it actually says.

Application of Scripture should always be made in light of sound interpretation. That is to say, the first question which must be answered is, What did this passage mean to the people to whom it was first addressed? After that question has been accurately answered, and then only, is it time to raise the corollary question. In the light of the original meaning of this passage to those people, what is God saying through it to us now? God's message today may not be absolutely identical with his message of old, but it will certainly never be inconsistent with it. In principle it will be the same; in application it will necessarily take into account our present situation, even as the original message took into account the situation of the original audience.

A final point is that the best application of Scripture is not the one the teacher makes for his class, for that may savor of manipulation, and certainly it can never be as meaningful as the one the members make for themselves. Curriculum plans and teaching plans should always make provision for the learner to make the appropriate application for himself. In this application of truth he may need some guidance; nevertheless, not too much guidance should be given. In the teaching-learning situation, we have to come to the point where we are willing to let the confrontation be between the learner and God alone. We must let the learner respond in his own way. We must be willing to let the Holy Spirit bring about the result which he has in mind. Anything else is unworthy of Christian education.

Whether we teach children, youth, or adults, the great need is for the message of the Bible to "come alive" in present experience. We must never surrender our faith that this can happen. If the Bible is what we claim it to be, then with the right kind of teaching, guided and empowered by the Holy Spirit, the written Word can become to the learner the living Word in the person of him who is God come in the flesh, even Jesus Christ our Lord. It should be the constant aim and prayer of curriculum planners and teachers so to work that such a result may come to pass.

Notes

1. See Holmes Rolston, *The Bible in Christian Teaching* (Richmond: John Knox Press, 1962). Chapter 1 (pp. 11-22) is entitled "The Indispensable Book."

2. *The Role of the Bible in Contemporary Christian Education* (Richmond: John Knox Press, 1961), p. 153.

3. *Teaching Ministry*, p. 25.

4. *Bible in Christian Teaching*, p. 22.

5. Wyckoff, *The Gospel and Christian Education*, p. 54.

6. Roland Bainton, *Here I Stand* (Nashville: Abingdon Press, 1950), p. 185. See also Rolston, *Bible in Christian Teaching*, pp. 17-19.

7. *The Church's Educational Ministry*, p. 484.

8. Ibid., p. 543.

9. The reader will note that these are also the areas which comprise the scope of the curriculum plan designed by the Cooperative Curriculum Project and set forth in the book, *The Church's Educational Ministry*.

10. See Colson, *Preparing to Teach the Bible*, pp. 45-63.

11. The summary of principles of interpretation given here follows closely the lines marked out by Holmes Rolston in *The Bible in Christian Teaching*, chapter 3, "Rightly Dividing the Word of Truth," pp. 36-47.

12. Ibid., p. 47.

13. *The Gift of Power* (New York: The Macmillan Co., 1955), pp. 182-83.

14. (New York: Charles Scribner's Sons, 1956).

15. *Teaching Ministry*, p. 149.

9
Leadership Training in the Curriculum

Curriculum, as defined in earlier chapters, is something which happens in actual learning experiences of real people. Although curriculum materials are highly important, they contribute to, rather than represent the essence of, curriculum.

Because of the dynamic nature of curriculum, the roles of teachers and other leaders are crucial. It is highly unlikely that the educational ministry of any church will rise above the level of its elected leaders. It is appropriate, therefore, that an investigation of the church's curriculum should include an exploration of ways to train leaders.

Any consideration of leaders in Christian education should begin with an acknowledgment of the essence of leadership itself. Basically, leadership in Christian education is a sharing of the Christian faith. It is one person, admittedly imperfect, who is used by the Holy Spirit to stimulate and guide the growth of other persons.

Thus, anything which contributes to the spiritual development of the leader is a part of his training. The congregational worship service, family and private devotional periods, efforts to win unsaved persons to Christ, and many other spiritually enriching experiences contribute to the effectiveness of the Christian leader.

Christian leadership is so complex, however, that leaders need additional specialized training. Especially do they need training in the content of the Christian faith and in the development of understandings and skills needed to help to guide the growth of persons entrusted to their leadership.

A church's first step in developing a comprehansive plan for training leaders is to select a director of leadership training. Ideally, this person should be a genuine Christian who has a good understanding of the objectives of Christian education, the learning process, the needs and interests of learners, and organizational designs and procedures. Inasmuch as it usually is difficult to find a person who possesses all of these qualifications, a church should choose the best qualified person available.

The director of leadership training should lead the church in developing a plan for discovering potential leaders. The membership of most churches includes potential leaders who are never considered for leadership positions. Many churches use talent surveys to discover potential leaders in their memberships. Although there is value in this approach, the word "talent" sometimes is misleading. Many people who possess outstanding potential leadership ability are not aware that they possess talents which would be useful in a leadership position. The term "interest indicator" might be more appropriate than "talent survey."

The data received on each person might be filed in a special folder. To this personal folder might be added from time to time newspaper clippings reporting the person's leadership in community activities, a record of training, and other data reflecting leadership potential.

If such files are kept on all members, church leaders will have a valuable resource for discovering prospects to fill vacancies when they occur.

The decision to approach a person about a leadership position should not be reached without serious contemplation and prayer. If God is to guide the educational program of a church, his help must be sought in selecting its leaders. Many "problem leaders" are the result of hasty decisions to fill vacancies. It is far better for a position to remain unfilled for a period of time than for it to be filled with the wrong person.

When the decision has been made to approach a person about accepting a leadership position, that person's training begins with the first contact regarding the position to be filled. The training of leaders might be thought of in three phases. They are preservice training, in-service training, and advanced training.

Preservice Training

Careful orientation and training prior to a person's entering a leadership position are highly important factors in determining success or failure as a leader.

1. *The invitation.*—The manner in which a person is recruited for leadership helps to shape an image of the position he or she is being asked to fill. Thus, careful attention needs to be given to the way a person is asked to fill a leadership position.

Normally, it is better for two persons to confer with a prospective worker at a time and place agreed upon in advance with the prospective worker. Not only do such advanced arrangements underscore the importance of the matters to be discussed but they also provide a safeguard against interruptions.

After a few moments of friendly conversation to establish rapport, one of the visitors might explain that the two have come on behalf of the church and after serious consideration and prayer about the matter they want to discuss. This places the invitation in context and helps the person to know that the dicision to ask him was not reached hastily.

The next step is to describe the specific work to be done. If the position is to teach a group of sixth-grade girls, one of the visitors should explain what the position is, who the girls are, and what is involved in teaching girls of this age.

The expectations of the church also should be explained clearly. If the church expects teachers to attend a workers' conference and to visit class members and prospects, these things should be made clear in the initial interview.

The resources which the church will provide also should be explained carefully. Special attention should be given to the opportunities the prospective leader would have for learning his new work and for growing on the job.

Finally, the recruiters should not press for a quick decision. It is fine, of course, if the prospective worker does accept immediately. However, if God has guided the visitors to approach the prospect, that prospect has a right to time for serious thought and prayer. It is usually better, unless a positive answer is received immediately, for the visitors to allow the prospective worker a few days to think about the invitation and to suggest that prayer about the response is needed. If this is done, it also is good to agree with the prospect on a time when one or both recruiters will call back for further discussion and, hopefully, an affirmative reply.

2. *Orientation.*—The orientation of a new worker is perhaps the most important single aspect of training. Leaders who are not given proper orientation but who are allowed to flounder and make unnecessary mistakes many times develop bad habits and discouragement from which they do not recover so long as they are filling the leadership position.

Many churches periodically provide an orientation course for prospective workers. The course includes such things as a general introduction to the educational program of the church, characteristics of various age groups, general approaches to age-group work, and observation of work with one or more age groups.

The opportunity to observe one or more sessions of the department or class in which one is to serve can be a valuable orientation opportunity even for prospective workers who do not go through a special orientation course. For such orientation to be most helpful, it should be done in three phases. First, prior to the observation session, there should be a general briefing session. During this period, someone, preferably the person who will teach or lead the group to be observed, briefs the worker(s) on specific plans for the session and suggests one or two things to which the observer(s) should give special attention. A second phase is the observation itself. Finally, there always should be an evaluation period during which the prospective worker is helped to evaluate what was seen.

3. *Installation.*—A third feature in the preservice training is a public installation service. If the church asks an adult to give generously of his or her time and talent to the work of the church, there should be some public installation setting that person aside for service. Not only does such a service give recognition to new workers, but it also is an opportunity for prospective workers to make a special dedication of themselves to the new work to which they have been called. This public recognition and "setting apart" can be a valuable and meaningful experience for lay persons.

In-Service Training

Many churches limit their leader training program to short-term courses offered periodically. Although the short-term course is one good plan for training leaders, there are other plans which are equally effective. If a church is to succeed in the task of training its lay leaders, it needs to offer a variety of training opportunities.

1. *Apprenticeship.*—One of the oldest forms of training is the apprenticeship. This plan has been used through the centuries to help persons gain the understandings, skills, and experiences needed to perform specific tasks.

The apprenticeship plan offers excellent possibilities for training lay leaders in a church. The term "apprentice" does not necessarily have to be used. Potential leaders can be assigned to work as associates to teachers and other leaders. While serving in this capacity, they can gain valuable experience which can help them to qualify later for full leadership responsibilities.

When this plan is used, apprentices should be given definite responsibilities. Some of these responsibilities might be performed in conjunction with the leader under whom the apprentice is serving. For example, an apprentice teacher might accompany the teacher in visiting class members and prospects. Through visiting with an experienced teacher, the apprentice can learn how to clarify objectives for visiting, how to arrange or schedule visits, how to establish rapport when visiting a prospect, how to deal with problems which sometimes occur while visiting, and other valuable skills.

As often as is feasible, the teacher should share with the apprentice plans for teaching specific lessons. The apprentice might even be asked to prepare certain learning aids to be used by the teacher. If the apprentice has been involved in planning, observing the class in session will be more profitable.

As the apprentice gains experience, the opportunity to teach the class himself could be arranged. When this is done, the apprentice should work with the teacher in developing a lesson plan and seek assistance in a post-session evaluation of the lesson.

Almost any church which uses the apprenticeship plan will have a core of leaders in training when vacancies occur.

2. *The process observer.*—From the field of group dynamics comes a plan which has possibilities for use in training leaders. It is called the process observer plan.

The process observer, as the term indicates, observes the process of a session and reports the findings later to the teacher or leader of the group. The director of leadership training might serve as process observer in some classes or groups, or process observers who are specialists in the work of each age group might be enlisted.

To provide maximum help, the process observer should have an opportunity in advance of the session to learn from the teacher or leader something of the plans for the session. The process observer then observes the session as unobtrusively as possible, making mental or written notes of problems encountered or the effectiveness of various aspects of the group session.

After the group session, the leader and the process observer sit down together and evaluate the session. The process observer might first invite the leader to tell how he or she feels about the session. After listening carefully to the leader's own appraisal of the session, the process observer might relate some of the good things observed. From that point, the observer might proceed to mention tactfully some of the features on which improvements are needed and suggest ways the leader might improve later sessions.

3. *The workers' conference.*—Most churches have regular monthly or quarterly conferences of their workers. Some of these conferences are department planning conferences. Others are conferences for workers with all age groups.

These conferences are training opportunities *par excellence.* Two features of the conferences have special significance for training. First, the problems discussed grow immediately out of the work. Therefore, as leaders engage in the discussion they are seeking answers to felt needs. In addition, normally there are opportunities seen after the conference for leaders to put into practice what they have learned.

Three types of concerns are discussed in most workers' conferences. Some time usually is spent discussing administrative matters. Even though some of these matters may seem to be routine, they can be presented and discussed in such a way as to provide valuable training to workers participating in the conference. For example, in discussing plans to visit prospects, the director might lead the group to share with one another some of the principles or techniques they use in visiting prospects. The director also could lead the group in role-playing a "teacher" visiting a "prospect" who is highly critical of the church. As conference members observe and discuss the way the "teacher" in the role-playing deals with the "critical prospect," they develop insights on how they, too, can deal with such problems.

In most workers' conferences, some time is normally given to curriculum planning. A director may not be able to sit down with workers individually and guide them in curriculum planning, but the workers' conference can be used as a means of helping workers know how to plan units of study and individual sessions.

Evaluation normally is a third aspect of a workers' conference. During this phase of the conference, workers discuss together the effectiveness, or lack of effectiveness, of past work. Periods of evaluation may be highly teachable moments, as workers seek to improve their work through an evaluation of past performance.

4. *Curriculum planning workshop.*—A curriculum planning workshop is a training activity in which workers meet together to develop under competent supervision their general curriculum plans for a quarter or for a year. Normally, it is conducted immediately after curriculum themes for the year or curriculum materials for the quarter become available.

The curriculum planning workshop is especially good for persons who work together in a children's department and for team teachers in older departments and classes. It provides them an opportunity to work out general plans for the quarter or year and to secure an objective evaluation of their plans from the director of the workshop and from other workshop participants.

One of the outstanding values of the quarterly or annual workshop is that it encourages workers to begin their planning early enough to select long-range goals and to relate individual units and sessions to these broader goals. It also encourages workers to plan and schedule a variety of outside activities. Workers who do this long-range planning discover in their normal daily experiences a wealth of teaching material which they would have overlooked had they not begun their planning as early as they did.

5. *Curriculum resource clinic.*—Two types of help are offered in a curriculum resource clinic. First, there is a careful interpretation of plans and resources available in the main-line curriculum materials. Through such an approach, workers are helped to gain an overview of the curriculum plans and deeper insight into the helps offered in the materials. In addition, there is provided a display of other helpful resource materials. Maps, books, audiovisual aids, and other resources are placed on display and workers are encouraged to browse around and find materials which they can use.

The media center director can be a valuable assistant in planning a curriculum resource clinic. This person can not only provide display materials currently in the media center but can also recommend other materials which can be ordered on request.

6. *Preview study.*—The preview study contains some of the features of the curriculum planning workshop and the curriculum resource clinic. In a preview study, teachers or group leaders using identical curriculum materials come together for a general preview of the content to be studied or taught. The preview can feature recommendations on resource materials and opportunities for workers to do some of their own planning for the unit or series of studies.

7. *Skill-development clinic.*—Some of the skills needed for effective leadership can be developed in one-session skill-development clinics. Examples of valuable skills which can be developed through this approach are how to use role playing, how to make friezes, how to operate a moving picture projector, how to keep class or department records, how to establish rapport when visiting a prospect for the church, and how to formulate good discussion questions.

In skill-development clinics, normally it is better to concentrate on one skill per conference. However, a church might offer simultaneous conferences dealing with a variety of skills.

The exact procedure in skill development clinics might vary, depending upon the particular skills for which training is being offered. As an example of one possible approach, the procedure listed below might be used in a clinic to help participants develop skill in formulating good discussion questions.

5 minutes— Leader explains the value of group discussion in learning

5 minutes— Leader discusses some principles for formulating group discussion questions

15 minutes— Participants work individually on formulating several good discussion questions

20 minutes— Participants share and evaluate questions which they have formulated

45 minutes— Participants "try out" a few of the questions which they have formulated and evaluate the strengths and weaknesses of each question

15 minutes— Participants take one or two questions used in the discussion and try to refine them to make of them better discussion questions

8. *Short-term courses.*—The traditional method for leader training in most churches is the short-term course. Although sometimes used when another approach would be better, the short-term course is an excellent approach to leader training if used in the right way. Normally, the short-term, teacher-directed course is a good approach in helping leaders to learn the content of the Christian faith. Short courses in various areas of Bible study, Christian theology, Christian ethics, Christian history, Christian missions, and church polity and organization have a valuable place in leadership training.

Two features can do much to increase the popular appeal of short-term courses. The first, and probably the most important, is the teacher's use of a variety of good teaching methods. So long as the teacher conceives of the task simply as reproducing verbally the content of the book, or lecturing on personal ideas on the subject, little real interest is likely to be stimulated. The teacher needs to establish meaningful teaching objectives and use a variety of good teaching methods in order to capture and hold the interest of class members.

In addition, careful attention needs to be given to the schedule for the course. Because of the heavy responsibilities of many adults, they are not able to attend a course every night for a week. Many of them would prefer either to stay longer the nights they do attend and to reduce the length of the course to three nights or to take the course one night per week for several weeks.

The adult education movement is demonstrating convincingly that adults can be attracted to short-term courses. Many churches need to reassess this method which they discarded several years ago as being unworkable.

9. *Renewal groups.*—Spiritual renewal groups are proving to be meaningful experiences for many Christians all over the country. In this plan, a group of concerned Christians meet together for a period of time to discuss their per-

sonal Christian faith and ways to increase their usefulness as Christians. Since anything which increases a leader's Christian faith strengthens leadership potential, the renewal group plan has possibilities for leader training.

10. *Denominational conferences.*—One of the best training opportunities available to church leaders is denominational conferences conducted on an associational, state, or national level. The leadership of these conferences usually is better than that which is available in a local church conference. In addition, workers from a church receive special inspiration and help by being associated with a large number of other persons who work with the same age group or who do the same general kind of work.

Although the denominational conference does not provide all of the training needed by church leaders, it is a valuable addition to the training which can be offered in an individual church.

11. *Media center.*—The media center offers one of the most effective means for training lay leaders. One advantage of the media center is that a competent and alert media center director can recommend books which relate to the immediate needs and interests of workers. Learning is more meaningful and lasting when it is related to the immediate problems and concerns being faced by the learner. The media center offers another special advantage in leader training. It is not always convenient for workers to come to the church for leader training activities. The books available in the library can be read at the convenience of church leaders in their own homes.

Advanced Training

Some churches are fortunate to have in their membership a few members with extensive academic training or professional experience. Sometimes there is a tendency to assume that these people do not need special leadership training to qualify them to fill positions of leadership in the educational program of the church. In most cases, this is a false assumption. Church leadership calls for specialized skills and understandings which are not necessarily developed through academic training and professional experience. A person may be an outstanding lawyer or physician without having mastered the skills needed to teach a Sunday School class. Although there may be occasional exceptions, generally speaking, it can be said that all leaders need to be involved in their church's regular leader training program.

It is true, however, that some persons with extensive academic training or professional experience may be challenged with specialized training opportunities in addition to those offered other workers. They may not find in the regular training program all of the intellectual or professional stimulation they need to continue to develop their Christian leadership skills.

A church can provide advanced training to such persons in at least three ways. One of the easiest and most effective of these ways is to place in the media center books which will challenge these persons to grow, and encourage these leaders to read these books.

Highly trained professional people who are leaders in their local churches need also to be encouraged to attend denominational conferences which will cultivate their Christian growth. Several of the seminaries are now conducting institutes for laypersons who are interested in advanced theological studies and social concerns.

Many lay leaders are finding university and seminary correspondence courses to be helpful. The Seminary Extension curriculum includes more than forty college-level courses in almost all subject areas found in a seminary graduate-degree program. These correspondence courses represent one type of study opportunity offered by the Seminary Extension Home Study Institute, Division of Extended Studies, Southern Baptist Seminaries. The address is Southern Baptist Convention Building, 460 James Robertson Parkway, Nashville, Tennessee 37219.

Finally, a church with highly trained professional people in its membership needs occasionally to have visiting speakers and conference leaders who will appeal especially to this group. Even though persons in this group may be in a minority in the church, they are an extremely important minority. They need special consideration if the church is to mean to them all that it should and if they, in turn, are to make their maximum contribution to their church.

10
Supervising Curriculum in the Local Church

If a church's curriculum is to attain maximum effectiveness, someone must give it wise overall supervision. The most fruitful teaching and training are never accidental. Intelligent planning of the total program is indispensable, and there is constant need for checking on progress and evaluating the results.

Problems affecting one or more phases of the church's educational effort frequently arise. These must be faced and settled in the best interests of the church as a whole. This calls for overall supervision. Furthermore, both teachers of classes and directors of departments need guidance and encouragement from an overall leader who represents the church in its totality.

The separate parts of the program must be correlated. Some churches have only an aggregate of separate and sometimes conflicting programs. What they need is a well-planned total program which is goal-oriented, comprehensive, balanced, and correlated. Unless curriculum is administered as a unified whole, the best educational results cannot be attained.

Even the finest trained leaders cannot insure the overall success of the program without total curriculum supervision. It is too much to expect a church to have topflight leaders in all of its educational units, and too often the best leaders are not wisely distributed. As a result, some phases of the work do not flourish. Even if all of the workers were persons of outstanding ability and training, there would still be need for overall curriculum supervision. The best workers do not resent such supervision; they welcome it, for they readily appreciate its value.

A Systematic Approach

Good curriculum supervision is one of the biggest needs a church faces. A systematic approach is called for. Slipshod dealing with a matter so important cannot be justified. The church must be made aware of the significance of its Christian education responsibility. If a systematic approach to the church's financial program is warranted—and experience proves that it is—how much more worthy of intelligent, Spirit-led planning and supervision is the curriculum of Christian teaching and training!

The proper group to make such an approach is the church council (or the Christian education committee in some denominations). Among Southern Baptists the church council functions as the committee on Christian education. Its membership includes the directors of the five program organizations, as well as the minister of education and the minister of music if there are such persons on the staff. Usually the pastor serves as chairman. Because the church council is composed of some of the church's best qualified leaders and because it represents the church's total program, it is the logical group to lay plans looking toward the supervision of the total curriculum.

A Curriculum Director

Adequate curriculum supervision calls for a competent curriculum director.[1] He may not be given that title, but his responsibility is to oversee and guide the church's total teaching ministry. He must either already have a good knowledge of the principles of Christian education curriculum or be willing to gain such knowledge through study and training. As the foregoing chapters have implied, competence in curriculum is a technical and many-sided matter; no one attains it without the expenditure of much time and effort.

The curriculum director, however, should be a person of more than theoretical knowledge. He must command the respect of the leaders of the various educational organizations. He must be capable of exercising strong, dependable leadership, of dealing effectively with people, of conducting his work in such a way that the church's program of teaching and training will be appropriately enhanced in the thinking of the total membership.

An important function of the curriculum director is that of bringing encouragement to all workers in the church's educational program. Morale is always a significant factor in church work; and the director who is alert to opportunities to express sincere appreciation for good work done, understanding of problems workers face, and hope when the going is hard, is an invaluable asset to the cause.

In some churches the curriculum director should be the pastor. The reason is obvious. Christian education is so vitally related to his total work that, unless the church has a minister of education, the pastor himself can hardly avoid the responsibility of being the active leader of its educational program. It must be said, however, that not every pastor is qualified by disposition and training to function in that capacity. Some pastors have given little attention to religious education and are not equipped to deal in the most competent way with curriculum matters. Some ministers think of themselves solely as preachers and pastors, and therefore they accept very little responsibility for leading their churches to become effective agencies of Christian teaching and training. But any pastor who is challenged by the needs and opportunities of curriculum direction in his church can, if he is willing to pay the price, qualify himself to exercise that direction.

In a church which has a minister of education, he will, of course, serve as curriculum director, this being one of the most significant phases of his total assignment. But in all such supervision, the minister of education is responsible to the church as a whole, the servant of the entire church and not just of certain of its parts.

In rare instances where a church does not have a minister of education and the pastor for some reason does not wish to assume the responsibility, a capable, consecrated lay person who has the respect and confidence of the church may be designated as curriculum director. Preferably he or she would be a person of professional training and experience in the field of secular education. However, if the person does not have such a background, he may yet take special training to equip himself for this specialized kind of service. The work of a curriculum director is not a task for a person without preparation.

Adopting a Curriculum Plan

Under the leadership of its curriculum director (pastor, minister of education, or carefully selected lay person), the local church should take formal action to adopt a curriculum plan suited to its needs. Most denominational publishing houses, especially the larger ones, provide more than one line of curriculum material, at least for some age groups. One of the reasons for this practice is that local needs and preferences vary considerably from church to church. Each church needs to consider its nature, its needs, and its goals, and on the basis of these facts adopt the curriculum plan or plans best suited to it. The size of the church, its location, the type of constituency it serves, and special problems which are peculiar to it are factors which must be carefully weighed before a decision is reached.

The curriculum director, of course, must take the lead in preparing for such action by the church. This will call for his own study of the various plans his denomination offers so as to become thoroughly acquainted with them. Also, he should make sure that the leaders of the church program organizations are well informed about these plans. This will call for personal conference with each of them about their respective parts of the total program. Finally, he should lead the church council or education committee, after careful study and prayer, to decide what is the wisest and best proposal on curriculum it can make for official adoption by the church.

In this connection a serious problem may need to be faced, a problem which causes considerable trouble in some churches. Occasionally teachers or leaders bring in materials which are out of keeping with their church's adopted curriculum plan. These persons have various motives for so doing. Some workers are actually at variance with their church's policy and wish to go their own independent way. In other instances, workers act on the advice of well-meaning but poorly informed friends who have led them to believe that these extraneous materials are better than those the church furnishes. The fact is that sometimes such materials are neither doctrinally nor educationally acceptable to the church's best leadership, and when they are used, actual harm may be done to learners.

This is a point which must be emphasized: *Teachers and learners have no right to use materials which are at variance with their local church's adopted curriculum plan.*

The curriculum director and the church council have full right to know and approve every piece of material being used in their church's educational program. Any worker who surreptitiously brings in material which is not a part of the adopted plan should be conferred with by the director of his program organization and the curriculum director of the church. He should be asked to cease using the material in question.

Once a curriculum plan has been adopted, the church should steadfastly abide by it. The curriculum director is the person to see that this is done. Of course, at reasonable intervals the entire plan should be reviewed and any needed changes or adjustments made.

Here again, the curriculum director needs to keep abreast of what the denominational publishing house is offering. He needs to study the pamphlets and brochures which are available explaining and interpreting its various curriculum offerings. He needs to be as thoroughly conversant as possible with the materials which are currently being used in his church. This he need not undertake to do by reading all of them through from cover to cover. But he can certainly thumb through them all on a regular basis. And he can have an understanding with certain capable and trusted teachers and officers that they will alert him to any problems they find, either in the teaching content or in the teaching and leadership suggestions of the various publications.

Occasionally there may arise the need to interpret to the entire church the curriculum plans and materials which the denominational publishing house is offering. At the least, such an interpretation needs to be made to the church council or education committee. Actually, the various members of the council or committee should study these matters personally. But in addition to that, it is good for the whole church to be reasonably informed about its curriculum so that it may take intelligent action when it is needed. This is especially true at those times when significant changes are made in the offerings of the publishing house or when there are changes of size, organization, grading, or administration in the local program of Christian education.

In many churches decisions about what line of curriculum material to use are not made by the best qualified persons; the ordering of the church's literature is done by a person who is really not sufficiently informed about educational philosophy and methodology. Such matters are too important for any church to be satisfied just to let someone order for the next quarter exactly what was ordered the last time. Yet that is the unfortunate way many churches do their ordering of church literature year in and year out.

The effort to help the church as a whole to become aware of the curriculum plans being used by its educational organizations brings some fine advantages. For one thing, the ministry of teaching and training is given the place of prominence it deserves in the thinking of the church. And then, where unjust and hurtful criticism of denominational materials is being offered, much can be done to offset or eliminate it. There is a saying that people are "down on" what they are not "up on." Surely it is the part of wisdom to help the membership of the church to be "up on" what is being done in its educational ministry.

The Work of Supervision

From what we have already said, it can be readily seen that the first requirement for effective curriculum supervision is an alert, dedicated curriculum director. Whether this person is the pastor, the minister of education, or a consecrated lay person, he ought to keep himself wisely informed about curriculum matters. First of all, he must constantly keep an alert surveillance of the needs, problems, and progress of the total educational program for which he has supervisory responsibility. And then he will need to keep abreast of developments in the general field of Christian education, as well as developments in the work of his own denominational program.

A church's curriculum director needs certain supervisory skills. Six such skills are discussed by Mosher and Purpel in their volume on public school supervision.[2] Although these authors are dealing with secular education, the skills they emphasize are equally important in the supervision of Christian education. They are: (1) *sensitivity,* that is, alertness to what is going on in the teaching-learning situation; (2) *analytic skills,* namely, the ability to effectively analyze emergent problems and their causes; (3) *communication skills,* or the ability to make oneself understood by the persons supervised; (4) *curriculum and teaching expertise,* that is, personal competence in educational planning and educational practice; (5) *interpersonal skills,* sometimes called human relations skills, involving such characteristics as personal warmth, empathy, as well as tough-mindedness; (6) *social responsibility,* based on well-developed concepts concerning the goals of education and their relation to society. Of course, it is not to be expected that every church will be fortunate enough to have a curriculum director who measures up to all six of these ideals. Nevertheless, every director ought to make a dedicated effort to develop himself into the most effective supervisor he can become. He owes this to himself, the Lord, the persons he supervises, and the church in which he serves.

Three of Mosher and Purpel's chapters are devoted to approaches to the work of educational supervision,[3] and each of the three approaches is also appropriate for use by a church's curriculum director. In each case the primary objective is the improvement of teaching. The first approach involves "planning for, observation, analysis, and treatment of the teacher's classroom performance." Thus the supervisor observes the teacher's classroom work, evaluates it, and on that basis gives the teacher assistance on how he may improve.

The second approach is careful personal counseling, which requires what the authors call a "colleague relationship" between the supervisor and the teacher. In other words, the supervisor must be responsive to the teacher as a person. In such counseling the aim is to help the teacher develop self-confidence.

The third approach is group supervision. Under this plan, groups of teachers meet together to share experiences and to counsel one another. The authors recommend six to ten as the right number of teachers for such a group. Of course, the supervisor presides over the session, but not to push his own viewpoints. Rather, his purpose is to help the group talk over their viewpoints, experiences, and problems.

It should be apparent that these techniques can be useful in some of the activities described in chapter 9, "Leadership Training in the Curriculum." (See particularly pp. 117-24.) The three approaches are not beyond possible use in a considerable number of churches. Certainly in the group approach and in personal counseling, the pastor can have a fruitful ministry of guidance and encouragement.

Effective curriculum supervision calls for regular meetings of various groups of workers for planning, training, and evaluation. Each meeting calls for a well-thought-out agenda, with a purpose and a goal. Some meetings will be for leaders of the separate organizations. Others will involve bringing together the directors of all these organizations, especially in the church council, for dealing with matters related to the churchwide program as a whole. The church council or education committee should be constantly kept informed of the status, progress, problems, and plans of each program organization. This group is the one which alone can correlate the operation of the total educational program and make suitable recommendations to the church.

Wise dealing with problems of leadership is also an important and time-consuming part of curriculum supervision. One aspect of this responsibility involves the church's nominating committee. This committee fulfills a major function in discovering the best persons to propose to the church for the various posts that must be filled in the educational organizations. The curriculum supervisor, therefore, is an indispensable member of the nominating committee, and he will help to guide its work in the procurement of workers.

One of the greatest leadership problems is the untrained worker. That person needs help. Sometimes he realizes his need; sometimes he does not. In either case it is not fair to this untrained person to expect him to do good work as teacher, officer, or leader if no provision is made for interpreting the task to him and giving him a reasonable amount of guidance as to its performance. Ways of furnishing the needed training include arranging to hold study courses, offering guided reading programs, holding personal conferences, and scheduling weekly or monthly workers' meetings. To help see that adequate provision of such training is made constitutes one of the chief tasks of the curriculum director.

Another problem is the uncooperative worker. That person, too, may need training in the worst kind of way but may not be aware of that need. Sometimes when the problem is pointed out to the worker, resentment develops. There are few things, however, that can hinder the teaching ministry more than the worker who refuses to cooperate with the plans of the organization or with the overall program of the church. If all efforts to secure cooperation fail, steps may need to be taken to relieve the person of that position. If the church elects its workers annually, such a person should not be nominated for another term of service. This, usually, is the easiest and in many ways the most satisfactory way to handle such a situation.

Still another problem of very serious nature is the worker whose morals compromise his leadership influence. When it becomes clear that such a compromise is actually the case, it is well for the person in question to be visited by the appropriate church officers. Every loving and earnest effort should be made to secure the offender's repentance and reformation of conduct. But if such efforts fail within a reasonable length of time, summary steps must be taken to remove the worker from the leadership position. As Paul well said, "a little leaven leavens the whole lump" (1 Cor. 5:6; Gal. 5:9, RSV). No church can afford to let a person of doubtful character continue to occupy a place of leadership in its teaching or training program. It is a case of "What you are sounds so loudly in my ears that I cannot hear what you say." Much harm will be done if the person is allowed to go on as a teacher or officer without a change of heart.

Strong Christian character and strong leadership qualifications are required on the part of a church's curriculum director if he is to cope wisely with the kinds of situations we have described.

Curriculum Supplements and Alternate Units

One of the important functions of the curriculum director is to discover and recommend for use in his church curriculum supplements and alternate study units. Sometimes the effectiveness of main line curriculum materials, such as quarterlies and books, can be considerably increased by the use of such supplementary materials. Of course, these are not ordinarily to replace the main line materials, but they do have a real function to perform.

Maps, teaching pictures, flipcharts, and audiovisuals may be mentioned as having good potential for increasing the value of quarterlies and books.

Maps are important because of the close relation between history and geography. Maps can make the study of biblical history much more meaningful. Teaching pictures, likewise, have value in making biblical incidents and teachings more easily grasped. Picture sets are regularly provided for use in children's departments, but they can also be helpfully used with youth and adults. Teaching pictures include both biblical scenes and present-day situations. Of course, teaching pictures should be carefully selected. They should be well suited to the age level with which they are used.

Another worthy educational tool is the flipchart. Flipcharts are effective in presenting concise summaries of informational or conceptual material. Since these aids are prepared specifically for use with a particular teaching-learning unit, they are usually listed on the publishing house's order blank in connection with the units to which they relate.

Such visual aids as flat pictures and chalkboards have been used for generations, and they are still among our most effective tools in teaching. A more recent development is the recording. Recordings of music, stories, conversations, and speeches can often be used to great advantage in the educational program.

Audiovisuals have come into prominence in all phases of education. Filmstrips which have an accompanying script or recording have the advantage of bringing their message through both ear-gate and eye-gate at once. Moving pictures have the additional appeal of action, and the sound track puts dialogue into actors' mouths.

There are right ways and wrong ways to use audiovisuals. When used with discretion, they can greatly intensify the effectiveness of teaching and training. Therefore, an alert curriculum director will help the faculty of his school to be aware of what is available along this line. He will help to provide appropriate films, filmstrips, and recordings as occasions arise for their use.

For several years The Sunday School Board of the Southern Baptist Convention has been preparing resource kits for the various units of study in both Sunday School and Church Training. Such kits contain a number of appropriate supplementary materials for the aid of workers—such things as posters, charts, maps, quizzes, fill-in exercises, and topic cards.

The curriculum director will also bear in mind the availability of certain alternate or elective teaching-learning units which can be of special use in meeting special needs. For example, a group of youths or adults in the church may have some special interest that would lead them to want to study a particular subject, possibly outside the usual time of meeting. Or a Sunday School class or an evening group will prefer to depart from the main line of curriculum materials in order to consider a subject in which they have more interest and from which they feel they will derive greater benefit. When the publishing house has materials already prepared for use in such a study, provision for such groups is, of course, much easier.

The choice of electives ought not to be indiscriminately encouraged, but often there is great wisdom in their use. Therefore, the curriculum director should be alert to discover special interests and needs among his people and be ready to suggest appropriate alternate units when he feels that their use would be justified.

Preview studies, which look forward to a coming unit or quarter of study, are also a useful tool to be kept in mind. Under good leadership, the preview of a set of lessons can prepare the persons involved to engage in later study with considerably more profit than might otherwise be true. Preview studies are especially valuable for teachers and leaders, though their use is by no means limited to them.

A Resource Center

Another responsibility of the curriculum director is to see that his church has an adequate curriculum resource center. By this we mean a place for storing and making available for use such items as lesson quarterlies and other periodicals related to the teaching-training program, also items such as books, maps, pictures, filmstrips, and recordings.

The best possible resource center is a properly equipped and functioning church media center. In fact, such a media center is essential to the best educational program. Modern translations of the Bible, commentaries, Bible dictionaries, atlases, study course books, and many other helpful materials should be bought, classified, and made available. A church media center has other uses besides its assistance to the educational program, but the importance of this latter function can hardly be overestimated. Fortunate, indeed, is the church which has a good media center and a good media center staff.

A useful media center setup does not come about accidentally. Persons of vision and ability must bring it to pass. One of these is the curriculum director. He will use his influence to see that a well chosen media center committee is elected, adequate budget provided, and the best qualified person chosen as media center director. Other media center workers should be added to the staff in accordance with the size of the church, the size of the media center, and other related considerations.

It is not enough, however, just to have a well-housed and well-equipped media center. Careful planning and hard work are needed to insure that its resources are used. Some churches have good media centers which are almost totally ignored by the persons who should and could be using them. In certain instances this condition is due to the fact that the persons in charge fail to see the media center's relation to the educational program and make little or no effort to help workers take advantage of available resources.

The media center staff must keep abreast of what is being studied throughout the various phases of the church program and then see to it that teachers, officers, and other leaders are made aware of the help the media center affords.

Some of the more progressive media center directors regularly bring to workers' meetings appropriate books and other materials which they can recommend to these workers for use in their various tasks. The persons responsible for such meetings must, of course, give the media center representative suitable opportunity to present the resources which were selected for recommendation. There obviously must be the closest sort of cooperation between the media center and the leaders of the church's educational departments. But thought and effort along this line will pay large dividends in the improvement of the teaching ministry.

Churches affiliated with denominations having a central media center service are fortunate, for this service can greatly assist in setting up and maintaining good media center facilities. The curriculum director should see that his church takes full advantage of this kind of help if it is available.

If the Curriculum Is to Succeed

Much of the success of a church's curriculum depends on the degree of appreciation the church has for the place of Christian education in its total task. Because teaching is such a vital part of the church's program, it is strange that members should ever fail to appreciate that ministry. Yet there is often a wide separation between a church's educational work and its other functions. Frequently the work of preaching and the work of teaching are allowed to drift apart instead of being recognized as two very closely related ways of communicating the gospel. Many persons seem to hold preaching in high esteem but give teaching only a place of minor significance.

Even some ministers fail to give their members engaged in the teaching ministry any sense of sharing with them in a common work. Many pastors, because of their own training for the ministry, are equipped to make available to their teachers and leaders excellent resources which could equip them more thoroughly for their tasks; but failing to see the opportunity, they do nothing about it.

At the risk of being repetitious, let us insist that the work of Christian education in many a church needs to be regarded more seriously by the membership as a whole. The majority of the members often have little sense of the importance of this task. And never will they gain the needed appreciation until the church's top leadership sets about teaching it to them. If the church is to be what Christ intends, this is a matter of high priority.

Here is one of the main responsibilities of a pastor. He must give adequate attention to the educational aspects of his church. He must help to interpret the significance of Christian education to the total membership. Such work is time-consuming, we grant; but if Christ's undershepherd is determined that his church shall fulfill its divinely appointed mission in today's world, such work is imperative. A great day has dawned for any pastor when he realizes that a worthy educational program with the right kind of curriculum, far from being a side issue in the church's work, is a major part of it and will do more to make the church true and strong and effective than almost anything else to which he can give his attention. When a pastor is convinced of this great fact, he is ready to help the church become convinced of it. And when the church is convinced of it, significant progress in the work of the kingdom of God will surely be made.

A minister of education, in like manner, must be more than an administrator; he must be truly an educator. That is, he must approach his entire task from a sound educational stance. He needs a philosophy of Christian education based on solid scriptural and theological foundations. He needs a good grasp of learning theory and educational methodology. He must understand and appreciate curriculum. He must never be satisfied just to keep the wheels of the educational organizations turning. His work is far more than just seeing that every class has a teacher. With clear insight into the significance of education and with a compelling vision of its potential for his church, the worthy minister of education joins forces with God as he takes his church where it is and seeks to move it forward to where he is sure God wants it to be. Such a minister will not only be a leader of leaders but, above all, a teacher of teachers. He will refuse to be the church's errand runner and insist on being its servant in the worthy oversight of all that is involved in good Christian education curriculum.

A Closing Word

And now just a brief closing word. This volume was written to help you gain a fuller grasp of your church's curriculum. The authors hope you now see somewhat more clearly what is involved in curriculum concept, planning, use, supervision, and evaluation. We began by saying that in a world of such tremendous changes as are now taking place, it is still true that churches must educate. They cannot be true to their nature or their mission without committing themselves wholeheartedly to teaching and training. Christ expects it and people need it. The gospel calls for it and the condition of the world demands it. Truly the churches must teach or die.

In all of this work, the outstanding need is for leaders who, with a clear understanding of the nature, meaning, and importance of Christian education curriculum, will give themselves to its selection and use with genuine Christlike dedication. The authors hope each reader is convinced that all of this is really worth the doing.

Notes

1. Here and in a number of the paragraphs that follow, "he" is used in the generic sense to refer either to a man or a woman. In many instances, ministers of education, as well as other curriculum directors, are women; and this is as it should be.

2. Ralph L. Mosher and David E. Purpel, *Supervision: The Reluctant Profession* (Boston: Houghton Mifflin Co., 1972), pp. 72-75.

3. Ibid., chap. 5, 6, and 7.

Appendix A

Elements in the Southern
Baptist Curriculum Design

Appendix A
Elements in the Southern
Baptist Curriculum Design

(Summary)

Introduction[1] (by Robert J. Dean)

The design and development of Southern Baptist Convention church curriculum plans and materials is the assignment of The Sunday School Board, Nashville, Tennessee; the Brotherhood Commission, Memphis, Tennessee; and the Woman's Missionary Union, Birmingham, Alabama. Extensive work by these agencies led in 1968 to a correlated curriculum for all ages. The earlier edition of *Understanding Your Church's Curriculum* (1969) reflected this cooperative work.

Additional work by The Sunday School Board led in 1974 to a *Curriculum Base Design*. This document related only to curriculum materials produced by The Sunday School Board—for Sunday School, Church Training, and Church Music. While not altering the basic concepts of the earlier documents, it added some new sections.

In September, 1977 a representative work group was assigned the task of updating the 1968 and 1974 documents. The work group completed phase one of this project in 1980. This work was endorsed by the Convention's program leaders through the Coordinating Committee of the Interagency Council. The materials in this appendix come from the *Church Curriculum Base Design,* 1980 update. The completion of phase 2 of the update project is scheduled for 1984. The final update will be based on a period of testing and evaluation of the 1980 work. If readers compare changes made between 1968 and 1980, they will find that changes have been minimal. This fact reflects, on the one hand, the quality of work done in 1968—work in which the authors of this book participated. This fact reflects, on the other hand, the desire of the project work group to base any significant changes on a period of testing and evaluation.

One goal of the 1980 update is to make the *Church Curriculum Base Design* a practical document for persons who design dated curriculum plans for Southern Baptist churches. The base design document contains curriculum theory and philosophy, but it is a theory and philosophy validated in practice. In this sense the 1980 update is less idealistic and more pragmatic than the 1968 work. The major goal in 1968 was correlation of curriculum. Southern Baptist churches had asked the Convention agencies to correlate their work at the denominational level, and the correlated church curriculum of 1968 was a response to that mandate. However, during the 1970s, diversity has been equally influential with the need for correlation. Churches want curriculum materials that match their distinctive needs. As Convention agencies have responded to a variety of requests, the result has been different curriculum plans and materials and several different lines of curriculum. Churches have been offered several options from which to choose in seeking plans that match their own sense of mission.

This approach is consistent with the understanding that Convention agencies have of their accountability to be responsive to the needs of the churches. Most churches do not have the resources to design and produce their own curriculum materials. Denominational agencies, therefore, design curriculum plans and produce curriculum materials to communicate the plans. The denominational agencies also seek to provide help as church leaders select and use curriculum plans and materials that are consistent with each church's understanding of its nature and mission. A church selects curriculum plans and materials, and enlists and trains leaders to implement the plans by using the materials. Curriculum is the result in learning that takes place in the churches. The denomination receives from churches evaluations of the plans and materials. These evaluations in turn shape future plans and materials. The following chart is designed to illustrate this process. (SBC in the chart refers to the three denominational agencies that produce curriculum materials.)

The *Church Curriculum Base Design* is for use by personnel in agencies of the Convention that produce curriculum plans and materials. This massive document is not designed for persons in churches who want to understand curriculum. The libraries in the seminaries of the Convention have reference copies for serious students of the subject; however, the cost and size, as well as the technical detail, of the documents preclude a church's using the eight volumes of the *Church Curriculum Base Design*.

This fact underscores the value of this book on *Understanding Your Church's Curriculum*, especially this appendix. When someone in a church wants help in understanding the theory behind curriculum plans and materials for Southern Baptist churches, that person is fortunate to have in hand a copy

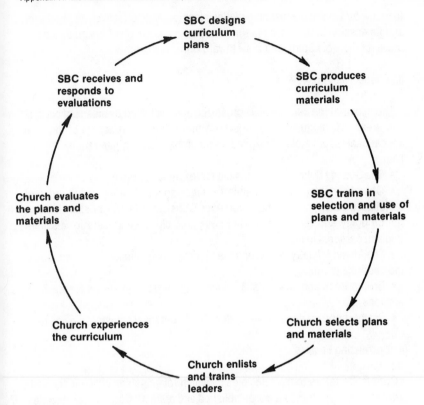

of this book by Howard P. Colson and Raymond M. Rigdon.

I. Objectives (See pp. 43-46.)

1. *Church—*
The mission of a church, composed of baptized believers who share a personal commitment to Jesus Christ as Savior and Lord, is to be a redemptive body in Christ, through the power of the Holy Spirit, growing toward Christian maturity through worship, proclamation and witness, nurture and education, and ministry to the whole world that God's purpose may be achieved.

2. *Educational—*
To help persons become aware of God as revealed in Scripture and most fully in Jesus Christ, respond to him in a personal commitment of faith, strive

to follow him in the full meaning of discipleship, relate effectively to his church and its mission in the world, live in conscious recognition of the guidance and power of the Holy Spirit, and grow toward Christian maturity.

II. Scope (See pp. 46-49.)

The scope of the curriculum is organized and explained by means of curriculum areas. Curriculum area is the term that refers to an aspect of the total educational responsibility assigned to a church program organization. Thus,

• The Sunday School is responsible for teaching the Bible.

• Church Training is responsible for teaching and training in the areas of Christian theology and Baptist doctrine; Christian ethics; Christian history; church polity and organization; and equipping church members for discipleship and personal ministry.

• The Music Ministry is responsible for developing musical skills, attitudes, and understandings.

• Brotherhood and Woman's Missionary Union are responsible for teaching missions.

• Brotherhood is responsible for developing personal ministry.

III. Correlating Factors

Correlation refers to the principles by which relationships between the various parts of the curriculum are established and defined. Correlating principles include factors held in common by all Southern Baptist curriculum-producing programs; they also include agreements about the distinctive areas assigned to each program (see above under II. Scope).

There are four key correlating factors:
1. Educational objective
2. Total scope
3. Learners in Southern Baptist churches
4. Methodology

Each of these factors is a broad category which can be broken down into more specific parts. And each of these parts can be broken down into even more specific parts. For example, the educational objective is broken down into "The Seven Objectives of Christian Teaching and Training," namely, (1)

Christian conversion; (2) church membership; (3) Christian worship; (4) Christian knowledge and understanding; (5) Christian attitudes and convictions; (6) Christian living; and (7) Christian service. These, in turn, are broken down into Age-Level Desired Learner Outcomes, which finally become dated aims and outcomes at the stage at which the dated curriculum plan is developed.

Similarly, the total scope is broken down into the five curriculum areas noted above under II. Each curriculum area is in turn broken down into age-level scope, which finally becomes age-level content at the dated plan stage.

Also, with reference to learners in Southern Baptist churches, curriculum planners develop statements of their understandings of the inherent capabilities (abilities and tendencies) of learners. These constitute two types of age-level readiness: (1) general age-level readinesses and (2) specific age-level readinesses. An important aspect of correlation is the way persons are grouped for learning in Southern Baptist church program organizations. All of these organizations follow the same overall grouping-grading plan.

Preschool—birth to grade 1
Children—grades 1-6 (ages 6-11)
Youth—grades 7-12 (ages 12-17)
Adults
    Young Adult—high school graduation or age 18 through 29 years
    Adult—age 30 through 59
    Senior Adult—age 60 through death

Finally, with reference to methodology, a lifelong learning task is stated for each curriculum area (see V. below). These in turn are broken down into continuing learning activities, and these into age-level learning activities. Then age-level methods are selected in keeping with age-level learning activities. The following questions are asked concerning every proposed method or procedure.

1. Is it in harmony with the educational objective?
2. Is it in harmony with the organizing principle?
3. Will it implement the lifelong learning task, the continuing learning activities, and one or more of the age-level learning activities of the particular curriculum area in question?
4. Will it be helpful in achieving the desired outcome of the particular unit of learning in which the group is engaged?
5. Is it appropriate to the age group concerned?

6. Is it relevant to the specific situation of the learners involved?

7. Can the teacher or leader handle it effectively?

8. Is it appropriate to the physical arrangements and resources in the local situation?

IV. Organizing Principle (See pp. 50-51.)

Our organizing principle is the involvement of learners in a meaningful exploration of the realities of the Christian faith and life in such a way that they move toward attaining the educational objective. This is done in the context of the church's life and work.

V. Lifelong Learning Tasks (See pp. 53-56.)

Bible (Sunday School): Seeking with growing interest and devotion to understand God's revelation through his Word and responding to him in faith, love, and obedience

Christian Theology and Baptist Doctrine (Church Training): Developing a valid system of Christian beliefs about God and his relationship to man

Christian Ethics (Church Training): Growing in Christian character and the ability to express it in every relationship of daily living

Christian History (Church Training): Discovering and appropriating meaning and values in Christian history

Church Polity and Organization (Church Training): Exploring church polity and organization and ways they guide Baptists in achieving Christ's objectives for churches.

Equipping Church Members for Discipleship and Personal Ministry (Church Training): Developing and dedicating to Christ skills which can be used in fulfilling the mission of the church

Missions (WMU and Brotherhood): Exploring with growing understanding the nature and implications of God's missionary purpose and responding to that purpose in personal commitment and obedience

Church Music (Church Music): Growing in musical understanding, attitudes, and skills and in the ability to express through music praise to God and witness to God, witness to the gospel, spiritual aspirations, and the joy and enrichment of Christian fellowship.

Developing Personal Ministry (Brotherhood): (The statement of this task was yet to be developed at the time this book went to press.)

VI. Age-Level Readiness (See pp. 61-62.)

Examples of some age-level readinesses which appear in more comprehensive statements are:

PRESCHOOL

1. They use their five senses readily in exploring their environment though their eye muscle development is incomplete.

2. They think literally far more often than abstractly.

3. They are ready for experiences which allow them to exercise both dependence and independence.

4. They are ready to give and receive love.

5. They accept simply stated religious truths without question.

CHILDREN

1. They are eager to make use of their abundant energy and rapidly developing physical skills.

2. They have some ability to express ideas, understand cause and effect, solve problems, reason, and plan.

3. They can accept simple rules, organization, responsibility, and leader-follower roles in group activities.

4. They are ready for increasing responsibility and opportunities for self-direction and independent thinking.

5. They are capable of experiences that involve feelings, imagination, deep thought, and choice-making.

YOUTH

1. They are ready for adult recognition and treatment in activities which call for maturity in physical characteristics.

2. They are ready to work hard for a sense of achievement and to reach chosen goals, both immediate and distant.

3. They go to extremes to gain the approval and companionship of their peers.

4. They are ready to commit themselves wholeheartedly and with great loyalty to a cause or person they deem worthy.

5. They can evaluate religious concepts independently and internalize those they find meaningful.

ADULTHOOD

Young adulthood

1. They are ready for activities requiring peak strength, vigor, and efficiency.

2. They are ready for serious training and expression of their mental capabilities.

3. They are ready to appreciate the value of relationships with others.

4. They can project themselves and foresee the possibility of fulfilling ambitions and goals.

5. They are ready to examine life philosophies and develop their own view of life.

Median adulthood

1. They are beginning to experience a decline in physical energy and stamina.

2. They prefer a type of learning that promises immediate value.

3. They recognize the symbols of success and seek success.

4. They are less willing than young adults to adapt to changes, especially to changes which do not seem to offer advantages.

5. They are capable of responding to the Holy Spirit with increased sensitivity.

Senior adulthood

1. They have decreasing physical strength.

2. They are reflective, cautious, and slower in their thinking processes.

3. They may be experiencing new social and family relationships.

4. They are more sensitive to reactions of others—kindness, affection, criticism, neglect.

5. They are more fixed in their religious opinions and attitudes and are either more responsive to spiritual truth or confirmed in its rejection.

Glossary of Terms

Age Division: One of the four major groupings of learners by ages: Preschool, Children, Youth, Adult.

Age Level: A selected span of ages grouped for convenient and appropriate curriculum planning.

Age-Level Content: The part of age-level scope that will be studied in a given time period.

Age-Level Desired Learner Outcomes: Desired results of learning for persons of an age level.

Age-Level Learning Activities: Expressions of a continuing learning activity that are appropriate for a given age level.

Age-Level Methods: Methods of instruction or kinds of learning activities that are appropriate for learners of a specified age.

Age-Level Scope: The part of the scope of a curriculum area that is appropriate for a given age level.

Balance: A characteristic of a curriculum plan that has neither overemphasis nor underemphasis of the various parts that make it up.

Church Program: The sum of all the activities a church engages in as it moves toward achieving its mission.

Comprehensiveness: A characteristic of a curriculum plan that includes everything essential in the scope and everything essential in the development of well-rounded Christian personality on the part of learners.

Concept Area: A broad concept considered appropriate for age-level scope.

Continuing Learning Activities: Those expressions of a lifelong learning task that relate significantly to learner needs at every stage of life.

Coordination: The process through which dated curriculum plans are designed in proper relation to other curriculum plans so as to enrich and reinforce learning for persons in the churches.

Core Curriculum: The part of age-level content that is essential for learners as they move through an age division.

Correlation: The larger principles and statements of relationships under which SBC church curriculum design is done.

Curriculum: The sum of all learning experiences resulting from a curriculum plan used under church guidance and directed toward achieving a church's mission.

Curriculum Area: An aspect of the total scope assigned to a curriculum-producing program or programs.

Curriculum Channeling: The process whereby emphasis program concerns are incorporated into curriculum as units and sessions are being designed and written.

Curriculum Plan: An orderly arrangement of subject matter and activities designed to facilitate specified learning experiences.

Curriculum-Producing Programs: The denominational programs that produce dated curriculum plans for use in educational settings in base program organizations of Southern Baptist churches.

Curriculum Materials: The media through which a curriculum plan is communicated.

Curriculum Planning Guidelines: The basic working document used in designing one kind of dated curriculum plan.

Curriculum Series: One of several distinctive approaches in designing dated curriculum plans and materials for specified program(s) and age division(s).

Dated Outcomes and Aims: Stated learning goals for a dated curriculum plan.

Dated Procedures: Methods and/or learning activities arranged in an orderly sequence and assigned to a given period of time.

Educational Objective: A statement of the ultimate end or intention of a church's total curriculum.

Emphasis Program: An SBC program that supports a concern or concerns which are interpreted and channeled by all appropriate church program organizations.

Focus Age: The target age or age group of a curriculum plan and curriculum materials.

Functions of a Church: Statements of intentions that should lead a church to do its work in ways consistent with its nature and mission.

General Age-Level Readinesses: The expected capabilities (abilities and tendencies) of persons at each age level which are an outgrowth of maturation and typical social experiences.

Intentions of a Church: A church's aspirations that grow out of its biblical foundations, understandings of human need, and philosophy.

Interprogram Coordination: The process through which curriculum plans are designed in proper relationship with curriculum plans produced by other programs for the same learners within the same time period.

Intraprogram Coordination: The process through which curriculum plans are designed in proper relationship with curriculum plans produced by the same program for learners in other age divisions.

Lifelong Learning Task: A meaningful, lifelong activity engaged in by learners.

Mission of a Church: A statement or statements defining the basic purpose for which a church exists.

Objectives of Christian Teaching and Training: Statements of learner objectives for each of seven aspects of the Christian way.

Organizing Principle: Rationale for relating the four key elements of curriculum design to one another.

Performance Activities: Congregational, organizational, and individual actions resulting from a program plan under church guidance directed toward achieving a church's mission.

Scope: Everything that is appropriate to be dealt with in the curriculum.

Sequence: A characteristic of a curriculum plan that arranges learning experiences in the best order for learning from the learners' point of view.

Specific Age-Level Readinesses: The capabilities (abilities and tendencies) of persons at each age level to become meaningfully involved in a particular curriculum area.

Tasks of a Church: Continuing activities performed by a church to carry out its functions and accomplish its mission.

Note

1. For the preparation of this introduction and for other valuable assistance in incorporating in the material which follows certain revisions which were made in the original curriculum base design, the authors express genuine appreciation to Robert J. Dean, Editorial and Curriculum Specialist, The Baptist Sunday School Board.

The authors also express appreciation for permission to quote freely from the updated curriculum base design in this appendix and in earlier sections of this book. *The Church Curriculum Base Design,* 1980 Update, has been endorsed by the Church Program Services Coordinating Subcommittee of the Coordinating Committee of the Interagency Council of the Southern Baptist Convention. © Copyright 1980—The Sunday School Board of the Southern Baptist Convention, Nashville, Tennessee. All rights reserved. Used by permission.

Appendix B

Christian Education: Shared Approaches— Goals, Theological Affirmations, Educational Affirmations

Appendix B
Christian Education: Shared Approaches—
Goals, Theological Affirmations,
Educational Affirmations[1]

CE:SA was developed by an interdenominational partnership called Joint Educational Development. An explanation of the system appears on pages 29-32.

I. Knowing the Word
  A. *Goal—*
  The goal of this approach is to enable persons to know the contents of the Bible, to understand their experiences and relationships in the light of the biblical message, and to recognize the tension between the truth of the biblical message and persistent concerns of persons and society, to the end that they may respond as faithful disciples.
  B. *Theological Affirmations—*
  1. Scripture is an authoritative witness for the church. The Holy Spirit inspired the authors and illumines the readers.
  2. The Old Testament will be interpreted historically, but applied in the light of the New Testament, which fulfills the Old.
  3. The Bible records God's revelation in Christ. It confronts persons with the promises and demands of the gospel for all of life, both personal and social.
  C. *Educational Affirmations—*
  1. Biblical content is the starting point of this system.
  2. Scripture is selected in an orderly fashion, taking into account the learner's ability to conceptualize.
    a. Stories for preschoolers are organized around biblical themes.
    b. Elementary children become aware of biblical themes as they emerge from biblical personalities and events.
    c. Youth and adults study Bible passages for meaning, with some attention given to application and interpretive skills.
  3. Methods suggested in the resources are uncomplicated, widely used, and refer to easily available materials.

II. Interpreting the Word

A. *Goal*
The goal of this approach is to increase the ability of the people of God to respond to the Scriptures, equipping them to be responsible interpreters of Scripture.

B. *Theological Affirmations*
1. The Bible, a book for the people of God, is normative for the Christian community. Each individual Christian is responsible, within the context of the Christian community, for interpreting the Bible so that it might inform contemporary reflection and action.
2. The message of the Bible, though culturally conditioned, transcends all times and places. No interpretation can be considered as final, but the experience of other times and other cultures can help gain insight into the biblical message.
3. A faithful reading and study of the Bible may result in a transforming encounter with God through the Holy Spirit, who inspired the writing of the Scriptures.

C. *Educational Affirmations*
1. Readiness to receive the biblical message is sharpened by interpretive skills, which can be taught and learned.
2. The teaching of these skills can be adapted to the needs and abilities of adults, youth, and children:
    a. Adults and older adolescents are at various levels of interpretive skills: Some need motivation to study the Bible; others need to acquire a disciplined method of Bible study; still others need opportunities to employ interpretive skills in a variety of ways.
    b. Younger adolescents and children can be helped to become familiar with essential biblical content and chronology that will prepare them for learning interpretive skills appropriate to adults and older adolescents.
3. The Bible nurtures Christian growth through the interaction of skills in biblical interpretation and knowledge of biblical content with a person's readiness to read the Bible as the Word of God.

III. Living the Word

A. *Goal*
The goal of this approach is to enable persons to participate in the life of the

Christian community and in its mission in the world as disciples of Jesus Christ, Lord and Savior.

B. *Theological Affirmations*

1. God, the Creator and sustainer of all, works among people and nations for their salvation through Jesus Christ. The approach draws from the biblical record, the experience of the church throughout history, and present-day perceptions of God's working. It probes the relationships among persons and with God in Christ to help persons discover who they are and what their human relationships mean.

2. Theology is faith in search of understanding, process rather than product, active inquiry, the responsibility of the whole church.

3. The Bible as the record of God's revelation confronts persons with the concerns of the gospel in relation to faith, values, relationships, social responsibility, hope, and discipleship.

4. The church is the people of God in Jesus Christ, sustained by the Holy Spirit, who sends it forth in mission, guiding and empowering its witness and worship.

C. *Educational Affirmations*

1. Learning takes place in the total context of the community of faith.

2. The sociocultural situation plays a major role in how persons develop and learn.

3. Learning is a function of the person's development, which is dependent on experience, perception and response, and maturation.

4. Individual differences require a variety of modes of learning.

5. Learners should be treated as subjects rather than objects.

6. Starting points for learning will vary, and include the gospel, personal concerns, and societal issues.

IV. Doing the Word

A. *Goal*

The goal of this approach is to enable persons to become increasingly committed to, equipped for, and experienced in participation in God's mission for the world, and to know both the joy and the cost of faithfulness in this mission.

B. *Theological Affirmations*

1. The good news of salvation speaks of God at work in the world and applies to societal as well as individual needs, with special attention to the oppressed and the powerless.

2. The people of God are called to discern how God is working in restoring humanity, restructuring society, and caring for all creation.

3. The church as a corporate body is called to witness by word and deed to the gospel as it relates to the pressing issues confronting society.

C. *Educational Affirmations*

1. Mission in society requires a firm rootage in a community of faith, whose relationships help foster intentional living.

2. Intentional living can be furthered through participation in a recurring process of awareness, analysis, action, and reflection.

3. Intentional living requires openness to the future. A Christian style of education should foster freedom to accept new experiences and cultivate the capacity to hope and to develop action strategies based on the biblical vision of shalom and reconciliation.

4. Persons and groups are at different levels of awareness and differ in their capacities for analysis, strategic planning, and action. These differences should be recognized and provided for with varying approaches.

5. Church education should help people become sensitive to the needs of others, to the reality of injustice, and to the need for changing societal structures that are dehumanizing. Educational strategies should reflect the fact that there can be no reconciliation apart from real progress toward justice.

6. The total life of the church should reinforce the relationship between the individual and corporate life. Common worship should reflect the church's corporate mission in the world while lifting up individual obligation and participation.

Note

1. This material, and related material in chapter 2, is presented here through the courtesy of JED. For additional information on Christian Education: Shared Approaches, contact Rev. John J. Spangler, Planning and Program Coordinator, Joint Educational Development, Presbyterian Center—Room 302, 341 Ponce de Leon Avenue, NE, Atlanta, Georgia 30308.

DATE DUE

9/13 4p			
9/17 2pm			
9/18 8pm,			
10/22 5:30			
10/23 1:30			
10/24 11:30			
10-24 4p			
11/17 9p			
4/7 9:00			
MAY 1 '89			
MY 9 '91			